HF
5686
.C7
L74

Lurie, Adolph G.

Business segments

DATE			

Adolph G. Lurie

BUSINESS SEGMENTS

A GUIDE FOR EXECUTIVES AND ACCOUNTANTS

DISCARDED

McGraw-Hill Book Company

New York St. Louis San Francisco Auckland Bogotá Düsseldorf
Johannesburg London Madrid Mexico Montreal New Delhi
Panama Paris São Paulo Singapore Sydney Tokyo Toronto

DEDICATION

To Warren Buhler and Susan Wagner,
who made this book possible.

Library of Congress Cataloging in Publication Data

Lurie, Adolph G
    Business segments.

    Includes index.
     1. Financial statements.   2. Cost accounting.
I. Title.
HF5681.B2L84   658.1'512   78-26808
ISBN 0-07-039113-0

1234567890   DODO   7865432109

The editors for this book were W. Hodson Mogan and Vir-
ginia Fechtmann Blair, the designer was Naomi Auerbach,
and the production supervisor was Thomas G. Kowalczyk.
It was set in Electra by Bi-Comp, Incorporated.

Printed and bound by R. R. Donnelly & Sons, Incorporated.

Contents

Preface

Early in 1976, I was invited to accept an assignment in Washington with the Commission on Federal Paperwork. Having recently completed my first book, I had been giving thought to some new major activity and felt this would be the answer to my problem. I telephoned the appropriate party in Washington, made a quick trip there, and shortly thereafter began a one-year stint as chairman of the study group on Segmented Financial Reporting.

The Final Summary Report of the Commission on Federal Paperwork, issued on October 3, 1977, included the following summary of the complete report:

Segmented Financial Reporting

Purpose and Scope. This report examines an emerging and controversial concept in business reporting to the Federal Government—a specific and detailed accounting by individual components or segments of a business enterprise. This departure from the customary practice of consolidated financial reporting for an entire corporate entity requires different accounting techniques and the development of new and complicated reporting systems. The report focuses on the Federal Trade Commission's Line of Business reporting program. The development of the program from the Quarterly Financial Report and the accounting and recordkeeping requirements associated with the LB program are examined.

Key Findings. The report finds that:

• Complicated and generally unavailable operational data are requested at great expense to business.

• Information requirements are poorly developed and produce information of questionable value.

• Confidentiality requirements are inconsistent, keep too much information from the public, prevent information sharing, and do not assure the confidentiality of business data.

- Poor communication between Government, industry and other interested parties prevents an accurate assessment of the value of business information programs and their costs.

- Present accounting techniques, including the use of the Standard Industrial Classification Code, are inadequate for providing the Government with useful segments of business information.

Nature and Scope of Recommendations. The report makes the following recommendations:

- An interagency task force under the auspices of the Office of Management and Budget (OMB) and the General Accounting Office (GAO) should develop improved classification systems to meet the segments of business reporting requirements of Federal agencies.

- The task force, consisting of interested Federal agencies, should work with representatives of industry and the Financial Accounting Standards Board (FASB) to develop the least burdensome segments of business reporting system.

- The FASB Statement of Accounting Principles 14 should be considered in the development of new segments of business reporting systems.

- The FTC should continue to assess and reduce the burden of LB reporting requirements as future developments in accounting standards and classification systems permit.

- Future changes to the LB program should include guidelines on the types of data entitled to confidential treatment.

- These guidelines should be developed in consultation with other agencies and interested parties and should provide the public with sufficient notice and an opportunity for comment.

When the project had been completed, it occurred to me that there was much to be said on the subject of segmented financial reporting that did not come within the scope of the Washington study. Many accounting, auditing, reporting, and management problems arising from the activities of the Financial Accounting Standards Board, the American Institute of Certified Public Accountants, the Securities and Exchange Commission, the Federal Trade Commission, and other government agencies were not covered by the study and its final report. Thus, the idea for *Business Segments* was born.

The objective of this book is to coordinate internal segmentation requirements, methods, and procedures with those required by the Financial Accounting Standards Board, the Securities and Exchange Commission, and other government agencies. Ongoing change in all these agencies makes it difficult to obtain any lasting guidelines concerning the many areas they regulate. Business use of segment data is not new, but the mandatory reporting of business is a relatively recent development and is in a constant state of flux. The more significant aspects are covered in the text that follows.

The requirements of management for performing its functions and evaluating results by segments are different from those now established by the FASB as generally accepted accounting principles. But with a proper accounting structure, both sets of requirements can be met within one system. I have endeavored to suggest how this can be done.

The SEC generally follows the FASB requirements for reporting to public stockholders. Other government agencies, particularly the Federal Trade Commission and the Bureau of Census, are more specific as to the lines of business and leave very little about reporting income and balance sheet items to the discretion of management. Some companies have little difficulty in complying with these agencies' requirements. Others find that their accounts are classified in such a way that they cannot readily furnish the information required by the government without undue burden. I have tried to reduce this burden by making suggestions for coordination.

During the Washington study, it became evident that three terms that were often used interchangeably needed to be differentiated to avoid confusion: *product lines* may be reported individually or grouped together to form *lines of business*; they may also be combined in other ways to make *segments of a business*. Accordingly, for the purposes of the Commission's study and for the purposes of this book, the following definitions have been used:

- *Product line* is an accounting term for classifying revenues, costs, and expenses related to a specific commodity purchased or produced for sale.

- A *line of business* is a classification of business activities for the purpose of facilitating the collection, tabulation, presentation, and analysis of data relating to business and for the purpose of promoting uniformity and comparability in the presentation of statistical data collected by various agencies of the United States government, state agencies, trade associations, and private research organizations.

• *Segment of business* is an *accounting* term referring to a component of an enterprise engaged in providing a product or service or a group of related products and services primarily to unaffiliated customers (i.e., customers outside the enterprise) for a profit. It is distinct from *line of business*, which is an *economic* term identifying groups of homogenous products or processes.

Adolph G. Lurie, CPA

WESTPORT, CONNECTICUT

Acknowledgments

During my work in Washington, I was impressed with many top-level bureaucrats and with their knowledge of business information statistics. These dedicated government servants were too many to mention by name, but I offer them all my thanks and appreciation for the help they gave me. I wish to offer special thanks to Warren Buhler, Executive Director of the Commission on Federal Paperwork, who assigned me to the project and gave me freedom of choice about how to proceed with my study. I also give special thanks to Susan Wagner, Assistant Director (Research and Special Studies), for all her help in guiding me through the complexities of the government toward the goal of the report to the Commission. In the preparation of this book, I had considerable help from the staff of the FASB, bankers, financial analysts, business executives, and other interested parties; they are too numerous to mention individually, but I would like to express my appreciation to them all. I particularly want to thank Charles Maurer, who reviewed the entire manuscript for technical matters and gave me much valuable advice. The members of the Alexander Grant & Company typing pool transcribed the many cassettes of material, typed the many pages, corrected my errors, and retyped and reproduced the manuscript in spite of their busy day-to-day schedule. Without their help, this book would never have been completed.

Last, but not least, my thanks go to Diana Lurie, my patient wife, who without complaining permitted me to mess up our den with cartons full of papers, books, pamphlets, and other material.

Adolph G. Lurie, CPA

WESTPORT, CONNECTICUT

CHAPTER 1

Development of Segment Reporting

In the beginning, business entities produced one general product line or performed one type of service. As the country grew, so did business, which expanded to meet the needs of customers and the profit motives of owners. Along came the industrial revolution and further business expansion and diversification, vertical and horizontal. With the advent of scientific management and advancements in the art of bookkeeping, accounting, and management reporting, the need for more data became apparent. This need was recognized by private business and the investment sector on the one hand and by the federal-government statisticians and economists on the other. However, each group followed a separate and distinct path.

Management initially was interested in recording the results of its activities and progress. But as management techniques progressed, there arose a thirst for knowledge of other companies' data for comparison. Financial analysts felt they needed more information of companies' segmented activities for comparison and for evaluating the status of publicly owned companies in the financial marketplace. This was particularly true as companies became more complex during the periods of expansion and the development of conglomerates consisting of noncompatible segments. The flowchart of the XYZ Company shown in Exhibit 5 (see p. 149) is an example of the interdependency of operations and transfer of products within an automobile manufacturing company.

Internally, companies needed segmented accounting information so management could assess progress and develop appropriate internal procedures for self-evaluation and of their diversified activities.

While this was going on, the government was far from standing still. Its needs were very great, but from a different viewpoint. Congress needed data to establish legislative controls for an expanding economy. Bureaucrats needed data to study the economy, make recommendations to Congress, and fulfill their legislated responsibilities. Congress was interested in statistics for making comparisons and in order to determine the needs of the country and make plans to meet those needs. Economists were hungry for data to assess the impact of government and private activities upon the economy and the marketplace. Congress passed legislation on the basis of economic and statistical data (including the various antitrust laws).

In order to enforce the laws, various agencies developed programs for obtaining information that would isolate violations of the federal statutes. This was particularly true of the Federal Trade Commission (FTC) in its studies of the major trusts, the concentration of markets and diversified companies.

A brief history of the need for and development of segmented business data for each of the two separate and distinct requirements of business and government can thus be seen by a capsule review of each.

GOVERNMENT

Bureau of Census

In 1902 the Bureau of Census (Census) was created to gather statistics about the population and to take the census as required by the Constitution. Through the years the Census became the principal data-gathering and reporting agency for the government, expanding from its initial responsibility of gathering data about the population to gathering all types of business and population data for use by government agencies and the private sector.

SIC and ESIC Codes

Early laws that had an impact on corporate record-keeping and accounting were the Income Tax Law of 1913 and the Federal Trade Commission Act of 1914. At that time, neither of these had any requirements for information by lines of business, product lines, or segments of business. Gradually various government agencies started to collect data in a minor way for their own specific needs. Recognizing inconsistencies in these statistical reports, an interdepartmental conference was formed in 1934 to examine the problem. In 1937 a formal interdepartmental committee studied the problem further, and during the period 1938 to 1940, the first edition of the Standard Industrial Classification Codes (SIC) was established. These codes enabled government agencies to gather, compile, analyze, publish, and disseminate statistical information with some degree of uniformity. The codes have been revised subsequently, with the last revision in 1972.

In 1963, the Enterprise Standard Industrial Classification Manual was developed from the SIC codes for gathering enterprise statistics as distinguished from the establishment statistics gathered under the SIC codes.

Securities and Exchange Commission

The Securities Act of 1933 and the Securities Exchange Act of 1934 resulted in the formation of the Securities and Exchange Commission (SEC) in 1934. This created another requirement for business data within the government. The Securities Act of 1933 is designed to provide for "full and fair disclosure of the character of securities sold in interstate and foreign commerce and through the mails, and to prevent frauds in the sale thereof, and for other purposes." The Securities Exchange Act of 1934 is designed to provide for "the regulation of security exchanges and of over-the-counter markets operating in interstate and foreign commerce and through the mails, [and] to prevent inequitable and unfair practices on such exchanges and markets, and for other purposes."

Quarterly Financial Reports

The need for more current information by product lines was developing. In 1947 the SEC and the FTC jointly started a Quarterly Financial Report (QFR) which has become the mainstay of product-line data reported by business and aggregated for distribution to all users of product-line data. The SEC gathered these statistics from public companies, whereas the FTC obtained the data from nonpublic companies. In 1971, all of this data gathering and reporting under the QFR program was transferred to the FTC.

World War II

During World War II, the Office of Price Administration obtained financial information for price control and the War Production Board gathered industrial information. These programs were later transferred to the Bureau of the Budget.

Corporate Patterns Report

As part of its data-gathering authority and for studies of concentration of markets, the FTC made a study of its data banks by industry and by company and issued a report in 1950 entitled *Industrial Concentration and Product Diversification of 1,000 Largest Manufacturing Companies*, which has been called the *Corporate Patterns Report* (CPR). It included data by industry totals according to the SIC codes. In 1972 these data were reissued, listing each industry with details of amounts reported by each company.

For 1972 the FTC initiated a program gathering similar data. In the future it proposes to gather and report such data every 5 years to correspond with the Bureau of Census Quinquenniel Census of Manufacturers. The FTC has issued a statement concerning the confidentiality of individual-company data to the effect that it will not publish individual company data pursuant to CPR 1972 earlier than January 1, 1978. This program is subject to litigation in the United States District Court for the District of Columbia between certain companies required to file there under the FTC.[1]

Internal Revenue Service

Since 1916, the Internal Revenue Service has been issuing an annual publication of facts deemed pertinent and valuable, under the title *Statistics of Income* (SOI). This report includes a vast amount of data obtained from the corporate tax returns and classified in part by lines of business according to Codes for Principal Business Activity and Principal Product or Service of Corporations which was based upon the ESIC codes.

Years of the Conglomerate

The 1960s can be called the years of the conglomerate. During this period there was a rapid expansion of business resulting from many mergers and acquisitions by corporations. This was encouraged to a great extent by the existing tax laws and by the securities marketplace, which looked with favor upon diversification. Hence companies acquired smaller entities that were not necessarily compatible with their other operations but would help the company grow, increase profits, and thereby increase the value of their securities on the financial marketplace. During this period there

[1] Master File 76-0126 (D.D.C.)

were many government hearings and studies concerning the effect of such activities upon the concentration of marketing power in fewer but larger companies. It was difficult to obtain appropriate information because the process of gathering statistics and aggregating data was such that the total for each reporting company was assigned to only the principal line of business, regardless of how significant other lines were. This resulted in considerable contamination of the important QFR reports and SOI reports.

LB Report Form

The FTC studied this problem and in 1973 sent out its first Line of Business (LB) Report Form to approximately 500 major corporations, requesting them to furnish data as to revenues, earnings, and assets according to almost 300 lines of business derived from the basic SIC codes. This program immediately became highly controversial and involved in litigation.[2] In November 1978 the United States Supreme Court ruled in favor of the FTC.

Some of the conflicts concerning the LB reports had spilled over into the government area. The responsibility for approving forms and data gathering from the private sector had been in the Office of Management and Budgets (OMB). The OMB had certain reservations about the LB program and withheld its approval. In 1973, as an amendment to the Alaska Pipeline Act, the approval of government forms for obtaining information from the private sector for 13 independent agencies of the federal government, including the FTC was transferred to the General Accounting Office (GAO), which had reduced authority compared with the OMB. It was after this transfer that the first LB forms were approved and distributed for gathering and aggregating the information desired.

Other Agencies

In addition to the Federal Trade Commission, the Bureau of Census, and the Internal Revenue Service, which were the more important purveyors of segmented business statistics, other government agencies obtained and aggregated data for individual needs. Although the Securities and Exchange Commission requires some business-segment reporting, it does not aggregate the data or publish any segment statistics.

The Department of Defense is interested in data of its principal con-

[2] Master File 76-0127 (D.D.C.)

tractors based on lines of business and in 1976 made a special study of 133 contractors. The purpose of the *Profit 1976* program was to acquire and analyze data regarding the profitability of defense contracts compared with commercial activities of domestic companies. The data collected and analyzed were used to study and perhaps change the profit policy within the Department of Defense with regard to awarding defense contracts.

In a similar vein, the Renegotiation Board has authority to obtain lines-of-business data in connection with its function of renegotiating government contracts in cases when it is believed that such data are useful to them in carrying out their duties. During the past several years, bills have been presented to Congress, including, among others, a provision making it mandatory for the Renegotiation Board to renegotiate government contracts on a line-of-business basis. These bills have never been enacted, but it can be assumed that a bill will be presented each year until a Congress feels strongly enough to pass an act making this and other procedures mandatory.

Regulatory agencies such as the Civil Aeronautics Board, the Federal Energy Administration, the Federal Power Commission, and the United States International Trade Commission may from time to time gather lines-of-business data for special investigations pertaining to their particular area of responsibility.

THE PRIVATE SECTOR

The history of business segment reporting in the private sector does not go back quite as far. Subjects related to this topic first appeared in the 1965–66 volume of the Accountant's Index, published by the American Institute of Certified Public Accountants (AICPA). Several factors led to the increase in interest in segment reporting. The large number of mergers and acquisitions during the 1960s and the formation of a large number of conglomerates with highly diversified activities were the principal causes.

Securities and Exchange Commission

Prior to 1968 the Securities and Exchange Commission (SEC) required filing registration statements showing a limited amount of information concerning lines of business. In the description of the company's business, it required a brief description of the products or product lines contributing 15 percent or more of the gross revenues, but it did not require any financial data. In July 1969, the SEC required financial reporting of the revenues by product lines in registration statements. In 1970, these requirements were extended to the annual report, Form 10-K. In January 1974, the SEC amended the proxy rules requiring the same data in the annual report as were previously included in the 10-K. In April of that year, the SEC indicated that it was closely following the activities of the Financial Accounting Standards Board (FASB) and that it would probably require compliance with any standard established by this organization. After FASB Standard No. 14 on Financial Reporting for Segments of a Business Enterprise was issued in December 1976, the SEC confirmed this position. In Release 33-58261, it proposed amendments under the SEC Acts of 1933 and 1934, which, if adopted, would require disclosure of financial information by industry and geographic segments. This was to be accomplished by amending Regulation 14A to require segmental information in certain proxy statements and in annual reports to stockholders and by adoption of a new integrated disclosure form called Form S-K.

In essence, the SEC's proposed amendments indicate acceptance of FASB Statement No. 14 and, if adopted, would result in elimination of the line of business disclosures currently required in many SEC filings. However, the SEC has proposed to expand the disclosures required by Statement No. 14 in several areas, as follows:

Dominant segment. The SEC would not give effect to the exemption in Statement No. 14 from presenting segment information if a company operates in a single or dominant industry. Rather, the SEC has proposed disclosure of financial information relating to a dominant industry if such segment has experienced a material change in revenues, market share, or profitability during either of the registrant's two most recent fiscal years. A dominant segment is defined as an industry whose revenues, operating profit or loss and identifiable assets each constitute more than 90 percent of related totals for all industry segments.

Intersegment sales. The SEC has proposed that additional disclosures be made concerning material intersegment sales and transfers. The following information (in addition to the requirements of Statement No. 14) is proposed:

- Identity of segments to which intersegment sales were made and amount of such sales

- Relationship of per-unit dollar amounts at which interseg-ment sales are consummated to per-unit dollar amounts of sales of identical products or services to unaffiliated third parties

- Percentage of total segment revenues comprised of interseg-ment sales

Five-year Information

Statement No. 14 requires segmental information for each fiscal year (or interim period, if required) beginning after December 15, 1976 for which a complete set of financial statements is presented. However, many present SEC forms now require information to be presented for 5 years and the SEC is proposing that segmental information be presented for the last 5 fiscal years. The issue of retroactive application in presenting segmental information for years beginning on or prior to December 15, 1976 has not been resolved.

Narrative disclosures. The new Form S-K requires registrants to describe each reportable segment of the business in the textual portion of appli-cable registration statements or reporting forms. The descriptions include matters such as the following:

- Competition

- Dependence on a few customers

- Backlog

- Sources and availability of raw materials

- Research and development

- Seasonality of the business

Foreign Operations

The narrative disclosures required by the new amendments also in-clude information about operations in foreign countries and the risk of such operations. Financial information about foreign and domestic opera-tions is required for 5 years if the registrant's foreign operations meet criteria set forth in Statement No. 14. However, the SEC will not require such information for years beginning on or prior to December 15, 1976.

Financial Accounting Standards Board

The accounting profession was not sitting quietly on the sidelines while all this was happening. During 1966 the Accounting Principles Board (APB) appointed a subcommittee to study the matter of disclosure by conglomerate corporations. In September 1967 it issued its statement *Disclosure of Supplemental Financial Information by Diversified Companies* in which it recommended "diversified companies to review their own circumstances carefully and objectively with a view toward disclosing voluntarily supplemental financial information as to industry segments of the business." In April 1973, upon the establishment of the Financial Accounting Standards Board (FASB), segment reporting was one of the seven initial topics for study by the new organization. The FASB issued its discussion memorandum in May 1974; received 144 position papers in connection with the memorandum; held hearings later that year; issued an exposure draft in September 1975; and received 233 letters of comments on this draft. In December 1976, after digesting this vast amount of material, it finally issued its Statement of Financial Accounting Standard No. 14 (SFAS 14) on *Financial Reporting on Segments of a Business Enterprise*.

Since the issuance of SFAS 14, communications were received from business executives and other interested parties which resulted in further action by the FASB. SFAS 18 was issued during November 1977 eliminating the requirement for segment reporting for interim periods. In April 1978 the FASB issued SFAS 21, retroactively suspending the application of SFAS 14 nonpublic enterprise. (See Chapter 12, "Recent Developments," for further details.)

Financial Executives Institute

The business world was also active while the accounting profession was studying this problem. In December 1966, the Financial Executives Institute, through its Financial Executives Research Foundation, retained Robert K. Mautz to direct a project on financial reporting by diversified companies. During the progress of this major project, several articles appeared in issues of *Financial Executive*, the Institute's monthly

TABLE 1-1
Classified Tabulation of Attendees

	Attendees	Speakers
Academicians	6	3
Attorneys	2	2
Business-association representatives	3	
Certified public accountants	10	2
Financial analysts	2	1
Government representatives	2	1
Industry executives	18	3
Stock-exchange officers	2	

magazine. The study was completed in May 1968, and a 390-page volume was published later that year.

National Association of Accountants

The National Association of Accountants also appointed a subcommittee of their Management Accounting Practices Committee and published *External Reporting for Segments* in 1968; A *Framework for Financial Reporting by Diversified Companies* in 1969; and *Financial Reports by Diversified Companies* in 1972.

The Tulane Symposium

Academia entered the fray in 1966 when a 2-day symposium was held in November with the Tulane Graduate School of Business Administration as host. Three professors of Tulane monitored the conference. The attendees and speakers were prominent persons from many fields of endeavor, as evidenced by the Table 1-1, above.

The papers presented and a *Synthesis of Discussion* prepared by Professors Alfred Rappaport, Peter A. Fiomin, and Stephan A. Zeff were published by Prentice-Hall, Inc., as *Public Reporting by Conglomerate* (1967).

THE MAJOR PROBLEM

The principal differences between the developments in segment reporting were the result of the different needs of government and of the business and the financial worlds. The government activities principally had to do with product lines and the markets for them; their objective was to aggregate the data from the many reporting companies so as to obtain meaningful statistics upon which decisions could be based. It was for this reason that the SIC codes and the related systems were developed and have been used by several government agencies in requesting data aggregation.

The purpose of segment reporting for the private sector is clearly enunciated in Standard No. 14, paragraph 5 as follows:

> The purpose of the information required to be reported by this statement is to assist financial statement users in analyzing and understanding the enterprise's financial statements by permitting better assessment of the enterprise's past performance and future prospects.

It goes on further in paragraphs 75 and 76:

> The purpose of the information required to be disclosed by this statement about an enterprise's operations in different industries and different areas of the world and about the extent of its reliance on export sales or major customers is to assist financial statement users in analyzing and understanding the enterprise's financial statements by permitting better assessment of the enterprise's past performance and future prospects. . . . Information prepared in conformity with these standards may be of limited usefulness for comparing an industry segment of one enterprise with a similar industry segment of another enterprise.

DEFINITIONS

It is quite evident that the data required by the government and the data required by the financial community are not completely compatible. Therefore, for the purposes of this book and to fully differentiate the concerns of the government as *lines of business* and the concerns of the business and the financial community as *segments of business*, these terms are defined below.

Line of Business. Generally an economic or statistical term referring to classification of business activities for the purposes of facilitating the collection, tabulation, presentation, and analysis of data relating to business, and for promoting uniformity and comparability in the presentation of statistical data collected by various agencies of the United States government, state agencies, trade associations, and private research organizations.

Segment of Business. Generally, an accounting term referring to a component of an enterprise engaged in providing a product or service or a group of related products and services primarily to unaffiliated customers (i.e., customers outside the enterprise) for a profit. It is distinguished from *line of business*, which is an economic term identifying groups of homogeneous products or processes.

CHAPTER 2

How Accounting Segments Are Used

GENESIS OF SEGMENT ACCOUNTING

A small enterprise with one manager, one product, and one market needs no segment reporting; in fact, it needs no management-information system because the information usually is in the mind of the owner-manager who can make decisions based upon personal knowledge. As the enterprise grows, so does the management group until the company reaches a state where it branches out into different products and different geographical areas, merges with other companies, and becomes more complex.

Management information systems with profit-contribution data of business segments have contributed to profit planning and results for all levels of management in multiproduct and multifaceted enterprises. The topic of this chapter applies to enterprises, both small and large, with a few product lines or with many divisions and products. An understanding of the uses of these data for internal and external purposes can help businesses comply successfully with the new requirements. Companies that have not utilized this management tool will discover its importance; companies that have prepared product-line data will learn how to update and improve their management-information systems. Readers of reports will be in a better position to understand the operations of the company they are dealing with if they understand the concepts involved. All will gain from what follows.

A management information system is created for the flow of data between the various elements of a business and the various elements of management from the lowest rung of the ladder to the chief executive officer. For internal purposes, segments may be devised in accordance with the management capabilities of individuals and the organizational structure of the company. Sometimes the division may be along market lines, production facilities, or production processes. At times it is according to the whim of top management and designed to satisfy the career requirements of the people the chief executive officer looks to for the success of the enterprise. In some instances, there is sound logic for the development of the segments; in others, they are derived from circumstances. Even if an attempt is made to establish segments on a logical and businesslike basis, internal political conflict may interfere; besides, circumstances change through the years, and top management often hesitates to make incisive changes.

MANAGEMENT USES

The Financial Accounting Standards Board (FASB) issued the Statement of Financial Accounting Standards No. 14 (SFAS 14) creating a great opportunity to review the entire segmental structure of an enterprise and revise it along more effective lines. The procedures suggested for selecting segments in SFAS 14 also create an opportunity to study existing segments, correct weaknesses, and strengthen strong points.

Any program to study business segments and their revision should recognize one very important factor. SFAS 14 was designed to provide for segment reporting outside the enterprise. Its purpose is to assist financial statement users in analyzing and understanding enterprises' financial statements by permitting a better assessment of past performance and future prospects. It is geared, to a great extent, to reporting to the readers of financial statements rather than to internal management. There is a vast difference between the two but they can be readily correlated.

For internal purposes, segmental data are an important aid for making management decisions at all levels and in all divisions. Internal information should be useful for production, research and development, marketing, budgeting and forecasting, and financial and executive management. With this in view, segment reporting has often followed the evolution of the management team. What is good for one company may not be good for another. As a company grows, it becomes more difficult to manage; hence segments are created to establish manageable units. Further growth may make certain manageable segments outgrow their individual structure, like biological cells, they are ready to divide in two.

A company might be segmentized by establishing divisions, each division being one or more profit centers for groups of related products. At one stage in corporate development, separate subsidiaries were established to handle different phases of corporate enterprise. The trend recently has been away from multiple subsidiaries.

The development of segments for internal purposes does not require outside acceptance by stockholders or auditors. It can be structured along the lines that are most useful for management. However, with the advent of SFAS 14, internal structure must be such that it can be readily utilized to meet the requirements of this statement. This should not be too difficult; segments established for internal purposes are usually well within the limits that meet the criteria of the FASB.

VALUE OF SEGMENTED DATA

Data by segments related to management personnel establish motivation for managers at various levels. Although production managers, for example, are most interested in efficiency of production and quality of output, they would also react favorably to knowledge of their contribution to the overall profit reported to stockholders. Without segmented management information systems, this is not always possible. Top management can use segmented data as an evaluation tool in searching out potential managers for the growing needs of the enterprise. The effectiveness of a manager at lower levels can more readily be identified and assessed with this tool. With an appropriate segmented management information system, useful profit models can be structured and compared with actual results. With these models it is easier to prepare budgets and long-term forecasts; more significantly, they can be used to determine the effect upon the entire enterprise of various alternative plans for future growth and for long-range planning.

Such models can also help in making decisions pertaining to future research and product development, the extent of employee training, and modification or discontinuance of products that reflect reducing profit contribution trends compared with those that show upward trends. This results in a more effective use of the resources of an enterprise. These various major significant items pertaining to segments for management purposes suggest certain criteria for establishing managerial segments beyond those required for reporting under SFAS 14.

MANAGERIAL SEGMENTS

It is quite obvious that managerial segments create a more detailed disaggregation than those required by SFAS 14. On the other hand, it does not require the same details as the Federal Trade Commission (FTC) Form LB report. It will be useful if the managerial segments are developed in a form that meets both external requirements.

To serve in both functions, reports prepared for each of the segments must be accurate and timely. They should be an integral part of the management information and accounting system. While it is preferable to establish these managerial segments so that accounting is at an operating-profit level, they can also be significant and useful if they merely report results at the profit-contribution level. The subsegments can be aggregated into the reporting segments required by SFAS 14 and the additional allocated costs and expenses applied to arrive at the operating level required by the statements. The uses for which management intends to develop managerial segments also influences the decision as to how to structure them.

For the purposes of reportable segments, activities at several locations may be combined when similarities of processes, products, or markets, are involved. For managerial purposes, each location may be a separate segment and hence be a separate cost and profit center. Through managerial segment reporting, the profit contribution or operating-profit activity is known at all levels of management. For example, production-department supervisors would receive the results of those products produced under their supervision. Plant superintendents would receive the statements of all the departments for which they are responsible. Plant managers would receive a statement of their plants and all of the departments and divisions reporting to them. Vice presidents would receive all of the data from all of the plants within their realm of responsibility, and all the underlying details would be available to them if they should desire to examine them. However, in each instance, the key report would be that on the top of the package, with the subsidiary reports supplied for further information if investigation is necessary.

In each instance, the reports at all levels should show the sales including intersegment transfers and all the corresponding costs and the net results. By this procedure, those on the production-line level can determine the impact of cost reductions or increased volume upon the profitability of their operations and their contribution to the entire enterprise.

USES OF SEGMENT ACCOUNTING

Uses for segment accounting are limited only by the capabilities of the management information system and the imagination of management in requesting the information they need and can use to make effective decisions. The following lists show some of the uses; they are not necessarily arranged in order of importance: what is important to one organization may not be important to another.

- To measure the effectiveness of management at all levels
- To develop management objectives and to measure their results
- To give top management the data needed for decision making
- To make decisions regarding continuing, increasing, reducing, eliminating segments or products or new segments
- To evaluate the effect of introducing planned new products or new segments
- For preparing budgets and accurate performance reports
- To measure the profit contribution of segments throughout the enterprise
- To measure the use of capital and the return on capital investments
- To determine the future financing and capital needs of the enterprise
- For comparison of different operating strategies within the company and to determine which strategies may improve the whole
- For long-range planning and projecting the effects of anticipated changes in the market
- To plan marketing programs and to measure their effectiveness
- To compare results with those of other companies as determined from their annual reports
- For comparison with industry results as reported in government product-line reports, trade association reports, and similar sources
- To isolate profitability problems and to determine whether they arise in production, distribution, marketing, or pricing, and which product lines they affect

- To plan pricing strategies

- To decide whether to make or buy certain units, plant equipment, or parts necessary in assembling production items

- To develop incentive plans and implement them on a knowledgeable basis

- For contractual purposes, such as payment of royalties, profitability payments under acquisition contracts, employment contracts, and other similar purposes

- For dealing and negotiating contracts with labor unions

- For complying with the Cost Accounting Standards Board requirements for government contracts

- For renegotiation purposes (the Renegotiation Board may require segment reports)

- And, to repeat, to give management at all levels the data they need for decision making on the many subjects that require their attention on a day-to-day basis

THE FUNDS STATEMENT

A Statement of Changes in Funds by segments is not required by SFAS 14. However, such a statement may be useful for internal management purposes. It might be rather difficult to prepare such a statement for managerial segments, but disaggregation of the Consolidated Financial Statements into reportable segments will furnish most of the information needed to prepare such Statement of Financial Changes at segment level. It is very useful for management to know which segments contribute to the increase of working capital and which segments are a drain. The procedures to follow to prepare such a statement vary depending upon the manner in which financial statements have been prepared, but it is strongly urged that such Statements of Financial Changes be prepared periodically to be used with all the other data that go into the management decision-making process.

BANKERS' USE OF SEGMENT DATA

Lending officers of banks have long felt the need for segmented data for evaluating and granting loans to major borrowers. For years, many borrowers have furnished their bankers with segmented data without benefit of the independent auditor's opinion. In some instances, the borrower offered the information voluntarily, in others, upon the lending officer's request.

Generally, the company furnished sales revenues and gross margin. Sometimes, the banks would receive profit contribution, but only rarely would they get operating income. In any event, this information, together with financial statements (which may or may not have been audited) and the bank's discussion with management were all used when the decision was made to grant the loan, and in determining the amount granted.

Segmented data assist the bank in evaluating the progress a company is making. The extent of diversification is an important factor. The potential profitability of each segment is considered valuable information, and is considered together with the intended use of the loan. The bank often has information about trends of various lines of business, and if the loan is to be used to bolster a fading segment, the bank might decline the loan or advise the company to change their plans.

Up-to-date knowledge of segment results and of the progress of the company in general is considered important data, even if the segments are reported informally. It helps the bank evaluate management, its major business decisions, and its future prospects.

In a survey made by the National Association of Accountants and reported and published in 1968 in *External Reporting for Segments of a Business*, it is stated that 56 of 70 bankers interviewed strongly favored contribution-margin reporting; the remaining 13 were generally unfamiliar with this form of income presentation and expressed mild approval or negative reactions. Some comments included reference to uses as:

- Can readily calculate the effect of planned use of borrowed funds

- Facilitates break-even analyses which are important to bankers

- Review of product mix in diversified companies

- Very useful; the breakout of fixed and variable costs is very important

- Facilitates the preparation of cash-flow projections

- Permits more sophisticated analysis of the reasons for profit fluctuations

- Break-even analysis is a key factor in seasonable business (segments)
- Useful in forecasting

Because banks have broad sources of business data, bankers also know much about the competition their customers might have in various segments and the portion of the market of a segment that the customer could get. Thus, a loan for entering a new market or expanding an existing product line can be evaluated more effectively with segmented data.

FINANCIAL ANALYSTS AS USERS

Financial analysts have been in favor of more disclosure and more information about companies whose stock is traded on Wall Street. The more they learn about the company, the better they can evaluate securities for investors, brokers, traders, financial bankers, and underwriters. Hence, analysts welcomed the requirements for segment reporting of diversified companies.

In an opinion survey of directors of investment research, conducted by The Financial Analysts Federation in 1972, 92 percent replied that they used segment information in their analytical work. Based upon this survey and other sources these data were used for evaluating.

- Earnings projections
- Company appraisal
- Comparison of growth rates
- Comparison of profit margins
- Risk factors
- Return on investment
- Rates of growth
- Multiple of earnings
- Impact of foreign operations

STOCKHOLDERS AND INVESTORS

The extent to which investors use segment reporting is not clearly discernable. In fact, the extent to which the average investor reads and understands annual reports has been studied and yielded only questionable results. Depending upon the degree of sophistication of the investor, valuable information will be available for investment decisions such as whether to buy, hold, sell, increase, or decrease holdings in a certain security. The extent of revenues and earnings in a specific industry could influence the investor reading the report. Suffice it to say that if it is available, investors can utilize all the skills just as professionals can: to the extent that they are capable.

SUMMARY

Complying with SFAS 14 initially would appear to add administrative costs to the operations of the company. However, there is more to be gained than lost by complying with these requirements and utilizing the resulting data. Management uses of the additional information obtained and the ability to make better decisions will result in gains that will many times offset the added costs.

CHAPTER 3

Accounting Problems—An Overview

There are a number of accounting problems which must be solved when meeting the new accounting principle promulgated by the FASB in SFAS 14. Other problems arise from the requirements for reporting lines of business to other government agencies. The more significant problems are summarized in this chapter. They will be discussed more fully in subsequent chapters.

Executives' understanding of segment accounting and reporting will be enhanced by this overview of accounting and reporting. It will help bring into focus the more detailed discussion of each subject later in this book. Furthermore, the overview helps clarify the relationship the several reporting requirements bear to each other. Similarly, accountants who must report on business segments and lines of business will be able to coordinate their efforts and be more effective.

SELECTING SEGMENTS

Of course, the most obvious and probably the more difficult kind of problem is the selection of segments that meet the criteria established by SFAS 14. For some companies, this will require a review and restructuring of some cost-accounting and financial-accounting procedures. In essence, the task requires a disaggregating procedure of existing financial data into segments. The SEC generally requires the same treatment.

All government agencies, with the exception of the SEC, request reporting data by aggregation, and reporting according to a derivative of the SIC codes.

The Bureau of Census prepares an *Annual Survey of Manufacturers* and a *Quinquennial Census of Business*, which principally require statistical data and very little financial data on an establishment basis.

The Federal Trades Commission has three basic reports:

- The *Corporate Pattern Report* which follows very closely the lines of business in the Census *Annual Survey of Manufacturers*

- The *Quarterly Financial Report* (QFR) which reports financial data according to 28 two-digit SIC codes; it aggregates and reports on the basis of enterprise information, assigning each enterprise to one line of business

- The *Line of Business Report* (Form LB) was first required for 1973; because of litigation and other problems, no data have been reported. Reporting is according to an Industry Category list derived from the SIC codes. The report requires segmented financial data consisting of profit-and-loss statement, certain assets and selected cost-and-expense items.

Approximately 500 companies have been required to complete LB forms. Many companies do not keep their accounts in such a way that it is possible to furnish these data in the manner required without changing accounting procedures or establishing separate records to aggregate the data as required.

Form LB establishes procedures for selecting lines of business, which involves selecting and aggregating components and meeting specialization ratios.

The SEC segment selection follows the SFAS 14 requirements with minor modifications.

The government agencies leave very little to the discretion of management, requiring conformity with established codes so that they can be aggregated into meaningful statistics.

SFAS 14 and the SEC give management considerable leeway to select segments that will give meaningful disclosure to readers of financial statements. SFAS 14 states: "Determination of an enterprise's industry segments must depend to a considerable extent on the judgement of the management of the enterprise."

SIC CODES

In most instances, the data required by the government for reporting under the SIC codes are readily available from the management information system of manufacturing corporations. The only reports requiring extensive data are the schedules in the FTC Form LB. In some cases, it may be necessary to restructure the accounting system so as to aggregate data within the company to meet the very stringent requirements of the FTC.[1]

In developing the segments according to SFAS 14, consideration must be given to maintaining accounting for each segment so that the independent auditors can satisfy themselves that the selection of the segments and the accounting for each are consistently in accordance with generally accepted accounting principles (GAAP).

REVENUES

In Form LB the FTC defines operating revenues as:

> The value (measured at invoice prices) of goods or services sold during the fiscal year) net of discounts, returns, and allowances.

The Form LB includes a separate line for reporting transfers.
SFAS 14 defines revenue as follows:

> The revenue of an industry segment includes revenue both from sales to unaffiliated customers (i.e., revenue from customers outside the enterprise as reported in the enterprise's income statement) and from intersegment sales or transfers, if any, of products and services similar to those sold to unaffiliated customers.

Neither definition addresses itself to the question of timing of recognition of revenues (such as cash vs. accrual methods), percentage of completion, FOB plant or customer's location; accordingly, it is assumed that the reporting can follow the accounting principles generally adhered to by the enterprise.

INTERSEGMENT TRANSFERS

The definition of transfers in Form LB is "the dollar amount of goods transferred or services rendered by one part of the Total Reporting Company to another part of the company. The same term is used whether the

[1] Reference is made to the table "Lines of Business Coding Structure," included in Chapter VI of Commission on Federal Paperwork, *A Study of Segmented Financial Reporting*, GPO stock number 052-003-00453-4, Superintendent of Documents, Government Printing Office, Washington, D.C. 20402.

sending or receiving parts are unincorporated or incorporated." The instructions do not require any particular method for valuing transfers and therefore it is appropriate to use the method generally followed by the company. Schedule III(C) does provide for reporting the percentage of the transfers valued at:

- Market
- Cost plus market
- Cost
- Other (specify)

This also implies that no single method must be used consistently. However, if there is any change in the methods used to value transfers, it should be indicated in Schedule V(D).

SFAS 14 is quite specific in paragraph 10(c) in stating that, "For purposes of this statement, revenue from intersegment sales or transfers shall be accounted for on the basis used by the enterprise to price the intersegment sales or transfers." In other words, follow the normal practices of the company in each instance.

The document goes on to define operating profit or loss as follows:

> As used herein, operating expenses include expenses that relate to both revenue from sales to unaffiliated customers and revenue from intersegment sales or transfers; those operating expenses incurred by an enterprise that are not directly traceable to an industry segment shall be allocated on a reasonable basis among those industry segments for whose benefit the expenses were incurred. For the purpose of this statement, intersegment purchases shall be accounted for on the same basis as intersegment sales or transfers (i.e., on the basis used by the enterprise to price the intersegment sales or transfers.)

Normally, internal transfers and related transactions are eliminated in the preparation of consolidated financial statements. Hence, the pricing procedures and amounts involved do not affect the final results as reported for external purposes. However, the requirements of SFAS 14 and FTC Form LB now require disclosure of these transactions and their impact upon each line of business or each segment of business.

The net income as reported on a segmented basis can be influenced by the policy established and the method used. Furthermore, changes in policy or method must be disclosed. Therefore, it is appropriate and timely to closely explore and revise past practices, if deemed advisable, so that intersegment transfers are reasonably priced, under the existing circumstances.

JOINT AND COMMON COSTS

The allocation of joint or common costs to lines of business as required by FTC Form LB is generally covered by FTC requirements for distinguishing traceable and nontraceable costs. The traceable costs are those costs and assets which a company can directly attribute to a line of business or which can be assigned to a line of business by use of a reasonable allocation method developed on the basis of operating level realities.

There are no instructions concerning the allocation of cost or operating expenses between traceable and nontraceable for Schedule III(A). The only expenses that are so allocated are media advertising, other selling, and general and administrative. It therefore is assumed that common costs in operating revenues are allocated in accordance with the judgment of management. The general instructions include a sentence as follows: "If the data required by the LB Form are not provided exactly in the accounting reports which are already in existence, reasonable, well-informed estimates should be provided by knowledgeable company staff." It is assumed that common costs of manufacturing can be appropriately allocated to lines of business.

SFAS 14 is more general in its treatment of the allocation of joint or common costs. In the first instance, it does not require much detail in the matter of costs since operating profit or loss is operating revenue minus all operating expenses. There are many ways to allocate joint costs, by-product costs and common costs. The method followed can influence the net income of lines of business or segments. It also can influence inventory valuations which in turn can affect the corporate net income. The consideration and treatment of the values assigned and the allocation procedures should therefore be studied thoroughly to result in reasonable justifiable methods.

LIFO

Those companies that utilize the last in, first out (LIFO) method for valuing inventories for financial reporting are faced with problems that are not discussed in any of the programs pertaining to reporting on segments or lines of business. It therefore will be necessary to reach a conclusion based on what is not said rather than what is said. The answer to the LIFO question is evident from the nature of the reporting rather than from the uses made by companies that follow this inventory valuation procedure for financial reporting.

For Internal Purposes

Most companies do not use LIFO for management control or internal reporting purposes but rely on first in, first out (FIFO), standard costs, or other allowable cost procedures. Via LIFO, the Internal Revenue Service basically grants companies permission to minimize taxes but with the stringent requirement that the same valuation method used for computing taxes must be used in the annual report to stockholders and in certified year-end financial statements.

On January 23, 1975, the IRS issued a release to allow companies adopting LIFO to adhere to the Accounting Principles Board (APB) and the FASB requirements by stating the reason why LIFO is preferable and by reporting the effect of the change on income for the year of the change only. The release also permits public companies to make the disclosures required by the SEC. As a result, this release by the IRS prevents violation of APB, FASB, and SEC disclosure rules.

It is rather difficult for a company to adjust inventories to a LIFO method monthly or quarterly for interim or management purposes. The LIFO pools are generally measured at the end of the fiscal year for income-tax reporting. At that time, the inventories are adjusted to LIFO pricing methods, and a reserve is usually established reducing the inventory to this method. At the opening of the books for the succeeding year, most companies reverse this reserve and maintain their inventories on their normal methods whatever they may be. Therefore, for internal management purposes, LIFO is seldom if ever used.

However, for interim financial purposes, it is desirable to follow GAAP and estimate the year-end LIFO reserve that is applicable to the inventory on hand as of the reporting date. Paragraph 14 of APB 28 discusses the appropriate treatment:

> Practices vary in determining costs of inventory. For example, cost of goods produced may be determined based on standard or actual cost, while cost of inventory may be determined on an average, FIFO, or LIFO cost basis. While companies should generally use the same

inventory pricing methods and make provisions for write-downs to market at interim dates on the same basis as used at annual inventory dates, the following exceptions are appropriate at interim reporting dates:

1. Some companies use estimated gross profit rates to determine the cost of goods sold during interim periods or use other methods different from those used at annual inventory dates. These companies should disclose the method used at the interim date and any significant adjustments that result from reconciliations with the annual physical inventory.

2. Companies that use the LIFO method may encounter a liquidation of base period inventories at an interim date that is expected to be replaced by the end of the annual period. In such cases the inventory at the interim reporting date should not give effect to the LIFO liquidation, and cost of sales for the interim reporting period should include the expected cost of replacement of the liquidated LIFO base.

Statement of Financial Accounting Standard 14

SFAS 14 makes no mention of LIFO inventory nor the treatment for the LIFO reserve. In the Introduction the statement says: "This statement requires that the financial statements of a business enterprise include information about the enterprise's operations in different industries, its foreign operations and export sales, and major customers." Please note that it refers to financial statements. Paragraph 6 states: "The information required to be reported by this statement is a disaggregation of the consolidated financial information included in the enterprises's financial statements." The consolidated financial statements of a company that uses LIFO for income tax purposes must also price the inventories on the LIFO method for the financial statement, and therefore the disaggregation of these data into sements must include inventories after the LIFO adjustment.

There is no serious problem for those companies whose inventories in segments represent separate LIFO pools. However, if the LIFO pools do not coincide with the segments, it will be necessary for the company to allocate the reserve for the LIFO adjustment on some reasonable basis. This would depend to some extent upon the mix of the inventory and upon the quantities and the dollars involved. One method is to allocate the reserve against the inventories on the ratio of the dollar value. A more complicated method is to determine the inventory reserve for each segment on the same basis as that on which the inventory reserve was computed on the entire inventory. Regardless of the method used to allocate the LIFO inventory reserve, the method must be followed consistently each year.

Securities and Exchange Commission

Since the financial statements reportable to the Securities and Exchange Commission are the same as the financial statements in the annual report, the result of any allocation for financial-statement reporting will be used for reporting to the SEC.

The instructions accompanying the LB form do not give any clue as to the treatment of the LIFO reserve for the various lines of business as reported in this form. In most instances, there will be more lines of business in the LB form than there are segments of business in the financial statement. Depending upon how the LIFO reserve is applied to segments of business, the same procedure can be used for reporting the various segments to the FTC.

No provision is made in the Summary Reconciliation Schedules—Schedule IV(a)—for adjusting for LIFO, and accordingly, the combined LB totals would be calculated after applying the LIFO reserve to the inventories. The only special information required for those companies having inventories on LIFO is the supplementary data in Schedule III(c). This schedule requires percentage of ending inventory valued according to:

- LIFO
- FIFO
- Average
- Other (specify)

Possible Alternative Procedures

Those companies using the LIFO method of inventory pricing can reduce or eliminate the problem if LIFO pools are considered when segments are selected. If it is at all feasible, it is easier to determine the LIFO adjustment as well as the reporting for each segment if the disaggregation of the financial statements into segments includes all the inventories that are in the same LIFO pool, or if no LIFO pool extends beyond one or two segments.

REPORTING PROCEDURES

The FTC Form LB requires considerably more data from reporting companies than SFAS 14. This can be discerned by examining the schedules to be completed. Not only is there no limit to the number of lines of business that are to be reported, more detail is required in the profit-and-loss summary (see Exhibit 2), and there is more information about assets and also supplementary data.

In addition, there is a schedule for reconciling the combined LB totals of the profit-and-loss summary and reconciling assets with either SEC Form 10-K or the annual report of the reporting company.

The key lines on the profit and loss summary of Form LB are:

- Total net operating revenues and transfers
    Cost of operating revenues

- Gross margin
    Total traceable other expenses

- Contribution margin
    Total nontraceable other expenses

- Operating income

Operating income for each line of business would be analogous to operating profit required for each industry segment by SFAS 14 except that general corporate expenses are allocated to lines of business in Form LB whereas they are not allocated to industry segments by SFAS 14. Furthermore, there could be many more lines of business in Form LB than segments required by the SFAS 14 limitation of 10.

Schedule III(B) of the LB form requires traceable assets to be reported separately from nontraceable assets for gross plant, property and equipment, accumulated depreciation and amortization, inventories, and all other assets whereas SFAS 14 only requires reporting of total identifiable assets by industries.

A company preparing the data for the LB report by disaggregating the SFAS 14 industry segments into individual lines of business or, contrariwise, aggregating lines of business to obtain segments of business, can readily reconcile the two schedules. Form LB requires summary reconciliations on Schedule IV(A) to reconcile the major captions of the report as listed above, and adding such items as nonoperating income and deducting interest expense, provision for income taxes, and others that might appear on the company's financial statements but are not reportable on the LB.

The reconciling procedure for each of the assets reported is accomplished by a separate column for each of the following:

- Combined LB totals

- LB adjustments

- LB reporting section

- Domestic regulated section

- Foreign section

- Consolidating adjustments

- Per 10-K or annual report

CONSOLIDATING PROCEDURES

The data reported on Form FTC-LB does not follow generally accepted accounting principles in the consolidating procedures. The FTC rules for consolidation are spelled out in glossary of terms used included in Appendix 1 of Form FTC-LB. The report form refers to the LB reporting section of the company which is therein defined. Consolidated domestic operations are reportable; they do *not* include the following:

- Foreign entities, either corporate or noncorporate

- Foreign branch operations

- Domestic corporations primarily engaged in foreign operations

- Domestic operations primarily engaged in banking, commerce or insurance

The report form goes on to state that "consolidation is optional for any domestic corporation required to file annual financial statements with the

Interstate Commerce Commission, Federal Aeronautics Board, Federal Communications Commission or Federal Power Commission." (These are referred to elsewhere in the text as regulated companies.) If the reporting company desires to consolidate these, it is "required to submit a copy of the annual financial statements filed with the respective regulatory agency." In most instances, it probably is easier for a company not to consolidate these regulated companies.

SUMMARY

It is evident that complying with the Federal Trade Commission poses more accounting problems than complying with the Financial Accounting Standards Board.

Exhibit 1, located at the end of the book, summarizes and compares the segments-of-business requirements of SFAS 14 and SEC with the lines-of-business requirements of the FTC Form LB.

For further information regarding intersegments, transfers, common costs, and reporting, refer to subsequent chapters.

CHAPTER 4

Intersegment Transfers

COST ACCOUNTING

Cost accountants have been dealing with accounting for transfers between production departments, cost centers, segments of business, among subsidiaries, and between parent and subsidiaries for many years. Each company made its own decisions, according to its own policies, about pricing these transfers in order to arrive at reasonably accurate costs of products in each cost center or accounting entity. GAAP was not a major concern of cost accountants since the most significant principles relating to them pertained to inventory pricing and amounts. Now a new dimension has been added by the issuance of SFAS 14 which establishes the importance of segment accounting, including intersegment transfers.

In the past cost accountants were only concerned with end results for each cost center. Interdepartment or intercompany transfers were usually eliminated before preparation of financial statements or in consolidating procedures. The auditor applied generally accepted auditing standards and considered generally accepted accounting principles for the financial statements taken as a whole, thereby coming up with an opinion that the statements were fairly presented without considering segment transfers or costing except for final inventory pricing.

Cost-accounting goals often are to determine the actual cost of producing a product or performing a service, but cost accountants are faced with many cost problems that militate against the cost precision desired. The problems now must be faced with segment-reporting responsibilities of the entity. Some of these are:

- Allocation of common costs
- The extent to which overheads should be included in costs
- Allocation procedures for overheads
- Estimates of spoilage costs

- Estimates of depreciation

- Estimates of power, electricity, gas, steam, and other utility costs, used by each product

- Last but not least, how to transfer costs between operating entities within the enterprise whereby one unit furnishes a product or service to another unit

Management's concern is to determine a transfer pricing policy for the enterprise, giving consideration to:

- How the company was going to manage each of its units

- How to report results

- Whether they should only consider the final costs of products that are sold to third parties

- Whether each cost center should stand on its own and have a normal profit on the goods that are transferred to another cost center of the enterprise

- Whether the transfer prices for products used within a particular division should be the same as transfers between divisions and subsidiaries

- Whether each separate department should receive credit for a portion of the profit of the end product sold even though the department only produces one component

It is not our purpose to solve these problems but merely to point out the more common procedures that are followed for transferring values of products or services, and to show what must be considered under the new SFAS 14 requirements for reporting operating income of segments.

DESCRIPTION OF TRANSFERS

For internal purposes, a company may transfer costs and services of a like nature that are incurred and accumulated in one account to other operating departments for the production of different materials. These costs can be allocated and transferred as required by the cost system.

A company may have items it produces in a particular section of the plant transferred to other production departments for use in their final products. The transfer price of these items is an amount representing a value considered appropriate based upon the number of units transferred to each department and is the source of the accounting transfer. These transactions may all occur within one company.

Furthermore, there should be transfer procedures when a company transfers semicompleted or completed products to an affiliated company. The procedure for pricing these transfers results from a management policy decision. In any event, in normal accounting practice, the final financial statements of a company or consolidated group as reported upon would eliminate these intercompany transactions as if they had all occurred within one company. The entries of the supplying unit are offset by the entries of the receiving unit.

In external reporting for segments in accordance with SFAS 14, each segment may include products from several departments or products from several subsidiaries. In reporting the results of a segment, a company must keep in mind the requirement that each segment report operating income as if it were a separate entity. According to SFAS 14 and also according to the instructions for FTC Form LB, transfers between segments or lines of business must be separately reported in the revenue section of the segment statement of the transferring segment.

For internal operating and accounting purposes, an enterprise can account for transfers within a segment. The accounting would offset the entries of the transferor and the transferee within the segment and therefore no external reporting is necessary.

REQUIREMENTS OF SFAS 14

As previously stated, SFAS 14 requires that transfer to other segments be reported separately; thus, each industry segment must report sales to unaffiliated customers separately from sales to other industry segments within the consolidated group.

FEDERAL TRADE COMMISSION LINES OF BUSINESS REQUIREMENTS

The lines-of-business requirements of the Federal Trade Commission usually results in more lines of business than segments required by SFAS 14. Schedule III(A) of the Lines of Business report requires that transfers to other lines of business must be separately reported before arriving at total net operating revenues and transfers. In Schedule V(B) provisions are made for reporting the total amount of transfers between LB's and identifying the transferring LB and the receiving LB.

Schedule III(C)—Supplementary Data—requires reporting percentage of transfers valued at:

- Market
- Cost plus markup
- Cost
- Other (specify)

These percentages are to be reported for each line of business. It is evident from this that the company may use whatever method it feels appropriate but that it must report what it is doing.

Unit prices can be assigned to each product transferred depending upon the management policy decision. In selecting a valuation procedure, due consideration should be given to the impact upon the operating results of the transferring and receiving line of business. Transfer pricing can have an impact upon inventory pricing of work in process, partly finished goods, and goods finished for sale. Any variation in these prices will have an impact upon the net profit as reported for segments of the business and the enterprise as a whole.

Different cost systems may have an effect upon the amount of cost attributable to each department and to each product that is produced, thereby having some impact upon the cost of interdepartment and intersegment transfers.

In "Financial Reporting by Diversified Companies," R. K. Mautz states:

> Probably no single accounting method lends itself so fully to the transfer of profits from one component to another, either intentionally or unintentionally, as does the pricing of intra-company transfers. For example, if component A ships partially finished products to component B, the price at which this transaction is recorded in accounts of the two components has a great deal to do with their relative profitability. An increase in that intra-company transaction price, for example, effectively increases the recorded profits of the shipping component A and reduces the profits of the component B.[1]

[1] R. K. Mautz, "Financial Reporting by Diversified Companies," *Financial Executive*, November 1968.

TRANSFER METHODS

A company may not want to confine itself to one transfer method, but it is desirable to be consistent from year to year. Based on the Mautz survey, 49 percent of the companies used one method, 23 percent used two methods, and the balance used three or more methods.

Cost

The easiest method to use, of course, is to transfer at cost. *Cost* may be defined differently in different companies. By this method, the shipping component credits its accounts with the cost of the merchandise produced, and the receiving component charges its accounts with the amounts transferred. In this event, the shipping component shows no profit or loss from the transaction, whereas the receiving component reflects the total profit accruing to the enterprise even though some of the production activities is elsewhere.

Market

A common practice is to have the transfers made at current market price for the goods transferred. How the market price is developed varies from company to company and may be based upon the average selling price of like commodities to unaffiliated customers. This method allows the shipping component to have its accounts reflect normal profit or loss and the receiving component to reflect the profit or loss resulting from its contribution to the production process and the sale.

Negotiated Price Between Components

The transfer price in this case results from negotiation between the management of two components within the enterprise. Some companies go so far as to permit a receiving component to obtain outside bids. If the receiving component can purchase a product at a lower price than from within the group, it is permitted to do so. This would put the affiliated unit in a competitive position with unaffiliated companies. On an overall basis, this is economically feasible, but it can be argued whether it is desirable. The answer depends upon the circumstances and management policies of the enterprise.

Cost Plus Fixed Fee or Fixed Markup

This is a compromise between cost and market. It enables an enterprise to allocate the profit or markup between components. The markup rate is arbitrarily fixed or may depend upon anticipated budgeted selling prices. Often the markup to market may be negotiated between the two components involved.

Other Methods

There are other methods used, developed according to the needs of an enterprise, each of which has merit in its particular circumstance.

One unusual method is to have the shipping component determine the transfer amount based upon market and record the intersegment sale accordingly on its accounts. The receiving component records the transfer at cost. The difference between the two amounts would be recorded on the accounts of the corporate office. In this procedure, the shipping component reflects its normal profit as if the merchandise were sold to unaffiliated parties. The receiving unit reports its profit or loss based upon the actual cost to the enterprise since it includes transfers from other units at cost. The corporate office would absorb the difference between the two as intersegment profit or loss. In the final consolidated financial statement, when the amounts recorded on all three units are combined, the net effect is to eliminate intercompany or interdepartment transactions.

SUMMARY

It is evident that the pricing of the intercomponent transfers for internal and external reporting is a complex subject. The methods followed and the pricing procedures used depend greatly upon the philosophy of management. It applies to the management of the individual components, from the smallest reporting component to the reporting segments as required by SFAS. Fortunately transfers between lines of business and between segments of a business can be priced by methods that the enterprise chooses to follow. The one requirement is that the enterprise to make full disclosure to the FTC as to what is being done and full disclosure under SFAS 14 of any significant changes.

CHAPTER 5

Allocation of Common Costs

Costs that have been incurred for the benefit of several or all operations of an enterprise need to be allocated on some reasonable basis to ensure that all components price their products and services to recover all costs, including common costs, and show a profit. Common costs may include coproduct costs, by-product costs, cost of centralized activities, corporate-office costs, and purchased services, materials, and utilities for more than one operation.

Executives at all levels should be aware of the influence of the accounting for common costs upon the total costs and upon the operations of each segment of the company. Due consideration should be given to the effect of alternative allocation methods upon the profit result of each segment and the resulting profitability rank of each product line. The new segment-reporting requirements make this more important and therefore management should reassess its present policies in the light of the external disclosure of profitability results.

DESCRIPTION

Common costs (sometimes referred to as joint costs) can include a variety of expenses and costs that are accumulated in cost accounting and financial accounting records. They fall into two broad categories: inventoriable and noninventoriable costs. Whether to inventory a cost or not is a significant problem; if not treated properly, it can affect the end results of product pricing, particularly when pricing is based upon cost rather than market. R. K. Mautz has demonstrated in his "Financial Reporting by Diversified Companies" (1968), that "the influence on segment net income of selecting one basis of allocating non-inventoriable common costs rather than another may change the rank order of reported segment net income and the rank order of rates of return on investment by segment."

INVENTORIABLE COSTS

Inventoriable costs are those costs and expenses that normally enter into a company's unit prices for establishing the value of an inventory remaining on hand as of any particular date. It would include direct manufacturing or operating costs or expenses such as:

- Materials used
- Direct labor
- Utilities
- Operating supplies consumed
- Factory overhead or plant burden

The factory or plant burden that is inventoriable depends upon a company's decision as to which elements of cost they desire to allocate to the different operations and product lines on some recognizable and realistic method. Depending on the company's method, some overheads may be a mixture of partially inventoriable and partially noninventoriable costs. The principal rule should be consistency in handling like overheads between accounting periods.

NONINVENTORIABLE COSTS

Noninventoriable costs and expenses are those which do not enter into pricing of inventory at the lower of cost or market. The most common are those expenses incurred in the corporate, home, or executive office of the enterprise. Noninventoriable expenses could be segregated as follows:

- Identifiable costs that can to some practical extent be allocated directly to business segments according to beneficial or causal relationship with the segments
- Cost and expenses that can be grouped into some homogeneous pool for allocation on a basis reflecting the relationship of the expenses to business segments including such centralized service functions as accounting, cost-accounting, purchasing, personnel, and similar departments
- Other that would be allocated to all segments on some consistent uniform method

The great variety of costs and expenses involved and the difficulty in determining and suggesting methods for accumulating and allocating such costs and expenses is recognized by the FASB, FTC, and other agencies that require segment reporting. They have not been very specific in requiring allocations to segments or lines of business and basically allow companies to follow the methods and procedures that they feel are most suitable for their purposes.

STATEMENT OF FINANCIAL ACCOUNTING STANDARDS 14

The FASB requires that an enterprise report its operating profit or loss, defined as its revenue minus full operating expenses. SFAS 14, paragraph 10(b), states that the enterprise's operating expenses that are not directly traceable to an industry segment shall be allocated on a reasonable basis among those industry segments for whose benefit the expenses were incurred. Paragraph 24 states that methods used to allocate operating expenses among industry segments in computing operating profit or loss should be applied consistently from period to period. It has been recognized that it is not practicable to distinguish between those operating expenses that may be said to be directly traceable to a segment and those that may only be said to be allocable. Respondents to a questionnaire pointed out that traceability often depends upon the sophistication of an enterprise's internal record-keeping system. They noted also that traceability depends on the degree to which management of an enterprise's operations is decentralized. In view of the problems cited by those who responded to the exposure draft, the FASB judged that disclosure of profit and loss contributions should not be required. SFAS 14, paragraph 78, does not proscribe such a disclosure if an enterprise wishes to include it.

The FASB continues to believe that certain items of revenue and expense either do not relate to segments or cannot always be allocated to segments on the basis of objective evidence, and for that reason the statement does not require that net income be disclosed by a reportable segment. Paragraph 79 lists such items as: revenue earned at a corporate level and not derived from operations of any industry segment; general corporate expense; interest expense; domestic and foreign income tax; equity or loss from unconsolidated subsidiaries and other unconsolidated investees; extraordinary items; gain or loss on discontinued operations; minority interests; and the cumulative effect of a change in accounting principles.

It is evident that some of the expenses incurred at an enterprise's central administrative office may not be general corporate expenses but rather may be operating expenses of industry segments that should therefore be allocated to those industry segments. According to paragraph 10(d), footnote 7, the nature of an expense rather than the location of its occurrence shall determine whether it is an operating expense. Only those expenses identified by their nature as operating expenses, shall be allocated as operating expenses included in industry segments operating profit or loss.

FEDERAL TRADE COMMISSION—LINE OF BUSINESS FORM

For those required to file the Federal Trade Commission Line of Business form, an entirely different set of rules applies. The reporting requirements include several levels of earnings, namely: gross margin, contribution margin, and operating income as reflected in Schedule III(A). Schedule III(C) provides for reporting a series of supplementary data for each of the lines of business for which operating income is reportable.

There are some major differences between these requirements and those of the FASB. Examples are:

- Discontinued operations should be reported in the same manner as continuing operations, that is, individual line items should be given for each line of business

- A single caption for cost of operating revenues would include all items whether traceable or nontraceable but allocated to each of the lines of business

- Media-advertising and other selling, general and administrative costs are reported separately as traceable or nontraceable, as the case may be

In order to meet the requirements of the FTC, it is necessary to reorganize the statement of earnings to meet the requirements of Schedule III(A). Traceable items are defined as those costs and assets which a company can directly attribute to a line of business or which can be assigned to a line of business by the use of a reasonable allocation method developed on the basis of operating-level realities. All other costs, expenses and assets are nontraceable.

It is stated that research and development costs could readily be attributable to lines of business and should be traced or allocated to these lines on the basis of reasonable criteria. Allocations in proportion to operating revenues are acceptable unless some alternative allocation basis seems more appropriate.

The schedule states that depreciation expense may be a component of cost-of-operating revenues, media-advertising expense, other selling expense, and general and administrative expense and should be traced along the appropriate expense category. In other words, depreciation should be included in each of the cost and expense items for the appropriate lines of business in Schedule III(A).

A number of items are excluded from the LB reporting section. They are:

- Nonoperating income

- Nonoperating expense

- Interest expense

- Basic research expense

- Research and development expense relating to lines of business in which the company has no operating revenue

- Provision for income taxes

- Extraordinary items

- Cumulative effect of accounting changes

- Minority interests

Reference is made to the Glossary of Terms furnished with Form LB for definition of most of the items. Nonoperating income and expense are not defined. Others are considered self-explanatory.

With respect to allocation of nontraceable expenses or assets to lines of business, the instructions state that a company should use the method it considers most appropriate for allocating traceable and nontraceable expenses or assets.

It is also suggested that the Cost Accounting Standards Board Standard 403 on the allocation of home-office expenses to segments are acceptable.

An effort was made in the design of the Industry Category list for FTC Form LB to avoid separate categories that share common costs with other related categories. This was done by combining SIC or Census codes into FTC codes to simplify the problem of allocation of such coproducts cost. For example, SIC codes 2016 (poultry dressing) and 2017 (poultry and egg processing) were combined into FTC code 20.02. A by-product must generally follow the principal product, and its revenue and total costs should be included with the principal product data. The instructions do not specifically refer to treatment of by-product data, but it would appear from the general procedures that it would be appropriate to follow the enterprise's normal procedures.

COST ACCOUNTING STANDARDS BOARD

The Cost Accounting Standards Board is a government agency whose stated purpose is as follows: "The Board shall, from time to time, promulgate cost accounting standards designed to achieve uniformity and consistency in the cost accounting principles followed by defense contractors and sub-contractors under Federal contract." It has issued a number of Cost Accounting Standards (CAS) of which the following are of interest:

- *CAS 402—Consistency in Allocated Costs Incurred for the Same Purpose.* The purpose of this standard is to require that each type of cost is allocated only once and on only one basis for any contract or other cost objective.

- *CAS 403—Allocation of Home-Office Expenses of Segments.* The purpose of this standard is to establish criteria for allocation of expense of a home office to the segments of the organization, based on the beneficial or causal relationship between such expenses and receiving segments.

- *CAS 410—Allocation of Business Unit General and Administrative Expense to Cost Objectives.* This standard is designed to provide criteria for the allocation of the cost of management and administration of a business unit based on beneficial or causal relationship. The standard also provides criteria for the allocation of home-office expenses received by a segment to the cost objectives of that segment.

The FTC refers to CAS 403 with respect to allocation of home-office expenses, stating that it is an acceptable method although not required. The standard sets a three tier identification procedure as follows:

1. Expenses are to be identified for direct allocation to segments to the maximum extent possible.

2. Significant nondirectly allocated expenses are to be accumulated in homogeneous pools and allocated on a basis

reflecting the relationship of the expenses to the segments concerned.

3. Any remaining or residual home office expenses are to be allocated to all segments. Residual expenses must be allocated in accordance with a three-factor formula which takes into account (a) volume or activity, (b) employees, and (c) invested capital. An arithmetical average of these factors determines the percentage of the residual expenses to be allocated to any segment.

ALLOCATION PROCEDURES FOR NONINVENTORIABLE COMMON COSTS

There are a great variety of common costs that are grouped in different manners by different companies. Similarly, there are a great number of methods followed by business in allocating each grouping of noninventoriable costs. Some of them are directly traceable; others may be partially traceable; and a great number are not traceable. The following are suggestions as to means that can be followed for allocating these costs, some of which may fluctuate according to the factors involved, and others of which are purely arbitrary and used for convenience. It is suggested that those methods be selected that serve management best for its own management information system and that arrive at the operating income for a business segment that management finds most useful.

Sales

A common method for allocating cost to product lines or segments of business is the ratio of the revenue or sales of the segments. Some common costs may vary fairly closely to the sales volume; among such costs are: selling expenses; marketing costs; and advertising, billing, accounts-receivable, and credit departments.

Assets Employed

Certain costs vary in about the same manner as the total amount of assets employed in a particular segment. This knowledge can be a useful tool in allocating such items as depreciation and amortization, insurance costs, and general maintenance departments.

Number of Employees

There also are common costs that vary approximately as the number of employees varies, as with personnel and payroll departments, fringe benefits, and first-aid facilities.

Massachusetts Formula

Because the Commonwealth of Massachusetts was the first to develop a formula for franchise tax purposes involving revenues, assets, and payroll, a similar formula has often been called by this name. It is used by several taxing authorities to allocate taxes within their geographical area. This formula can also be used for allocating general costs not reasonably allocable by any other manner.

The formula is simple to apply. Three percentages are computed and an arithmetic average is taken to arrive at a single percentage for allocation purposes. The three percentages are:

1. The percentage of sales for the segment to the total sales of the enterprise

2. Percentage of the gross payroll of the segment related to the gross payroll of the enterprise

3. Percentage of total assets of the segment to total assets of the enterprise

The total of the average percentages for all segments equals 100 percent as shown in Table 5-1.

TABLE 5-1
Average Percentages of Segments

	Sales amount	Percent	Payroll amount	Percent	Assets amount	Percent	Average percent
Segment A	$ 5,000	50	$ 400	40	$ 900	45	45
Segment B	3,000	30	500	50	800	40	40
Segment C	2,000	20	100	10	300	15	15
Total enterprise	$10,000	100%	$1,000	100%	$2,000	100%	100%

Using this formula, common costs would be allocated to:

- Segment A   45%
- Segment B   40%
- Segment C   15%

Gross Profits

Gross profits representing net revenues less direct cost of the revenues can be used as a base for allocating common costs and expenses. This has the advantage of reporting net income on a basis that is controllable by production management. Furthermore, it is easy to apply.

Other Methods

Many other suggestions can be made. Management, accounting staff, and the cost department can find procedures and supply reasons for using or not using each and every one. It is suggested that each enterprise study its own problems and develop its own theories and procedures for allocating costs, either for groups or individual common costs, that best serve their internal operating purposes. These can be used for reporting segments of their business in their annual reports or for reporting to those government agencies requiring such information.

CHARGING COST CENTERS

For internal control purposes, a procedure is required for charging the allocated amount or amounts for interim period accounting. To be effective, the management of an enterprise should receive operating income or income contribution statements for each product line, department, business segment, or operating unit periodically, that is, monthly or quarterly, as best suits their purposes.

It does not matter whether one or more allocation procedures mentioned above are used, but one method seems to be fairly prevalent and is relatively easy to apply. Based upon past experience or the current year's budget, a percentage is computed for charging each operational or control unit. This percentage is computed for and applied to any one of the following amounts consistently throughout the enterprise:

- The capital utilization of each unit usually representing the total assets (the sum of costs, inventories, accounts receivable, fixed assets, etc.)

- Net working capital of each unit

- Net working current assets of each unit (cash, inventories, and accounts receivable)

- Any other basis that appears appropriate and reasonable to management as a means of allocating common costs

SUMMARY

No two companies accumulate costs in exactly the same fashion. Enterprises allocate costs to segments of business, lines of business, cost centers, divisions, or any other unit that may be useful for their purposes. Accordingly, they must consider what they can best use, develop it, and refine it for their own purposes. A cardinal rule could require that a degree of consistency between periods and among segments be maintained so that reasonable comparisons can be made. Regardless of what procedure is followed, not everyone will be happy with the allocation procedures or results. Just be reasonable and do your best, and a useful, appropriate data-gathering system will result that will contribute to your company's knowledge of its operations and decision making in an effective manner.

CHAPTER 6

Government Requirements for Lines of Business Data

An enterprise may not be required to file FTC Form LB (which pertains to about 500 of the country's largest corporations) or to complete the FTC/QFR report (required from a sample of about 12,000 corporations), but its management should know the extent of the government's activity in this data gathering and reporting field. These activities may increase and more companies may be involved.

However, more important are the reports issued by the agencies. These reports include a vast amount of valuable information that management can use in making comparative evaluations of their own operations. They also include helpful tools for making many decisions on such matters as size of markets, industry-wide financial statements, and the like.

A *line of business* has been defined as a "classification of business activities for the purpose of facilitating the collection, tabulation, presentation, and analysis of data relating to business; and for promoting uniformity and comparability in the presentation of statistical data collected by various agencies of the United States Government, state agencies, trade associations, and private research organizations.[1] In some instances, the term *product line* has been used to mean the same thing.

CODES

SIC and ESIC Codes

Government agencies have taken the SIC Codes and modified them for their own purposes. There are over 1000 product lines in the SIC Codes. The above definition of *line of business* is quite similar to the definition in the SIC Codes, which refers to "data relating to establishments" rather

---

[1] "A Study of Segmented Financial Reporting," A *Staff Report to the Commission on Federal Paperwork*, Washington, D.C., May 1977.

than to business. The key word that requires clarification is *establishment*. An establishment is defined as an economic unit, generally at a single physical location where business is conducted or where services or industrial operations are performed (for example a factory, mill, store, hotel, movie theater, mine, farm, ranch, bank, railroad depot, airline terminal, sales office, warehouse, or central administrative office). The SIC Code, a volume of 649 pages, is prepared and published by the Office of Management and Budget (OMB). The codification is by 11 divisions, each identified by a letter. Each division is divided into major groups, which are identified by two-digit numbers. A third digit identifies subgroups. A fourth digit is added to identify one or more industries within each group. Each industry is described in a short paragraph that includes a list of the industry's more common products. The resulting volume contains more than 1000 four-digit codes.

Different codes have been developed from the SIC Codes for specific purposes, the most common being the Enterprise Standard Industrial Classification System (ESIC). Recognizing that the establishment characteristics of SIC did not meet all needs, the OMB created the ESIC in 1963. Its purpose is to provide a standard for use with the statistics about enterprises (i.e., companies rather than their individual establishments) according to their economic activity. As stated in the ESIC Manual, "its use is to facilitate the collection, tabulation, presentation, uniformity and comparability in the statistical data of federal government agencies. The classification of enterprises, rather than their constituent establishment, is used for compiling and analyzing financial and related statistics (such as income, expenses, and profits from the income statement; debt, liquidity, and other balance sheet items; and other data that only may be available on an enterprise basis)."[2] The ESIC Manual Code consists of approximately 250 codes. The Manual provides a cross-reference between the SIC and ESIC. It uses a two-, three-, or four-digit code. For identification and to distinguish it from the SIC code, the ESIC code has a decimal point between the first two digits or between the third and fourth digits.

Bureau of Census Codes

The Bureau of Census (Census) gathers and reports on a vast amount of statistics in its Census of Manufacturers, conducted every 5 years, and in its Annual Survey of Manufacturers, and has expanded the SIC Code. Its

[2] *Enterprise Standard Industrial Classification Manual*, 1974, p. 34

code consists of approximately 450 industries, 1,300 product codes and 11,000 products reported by establishments.

Federal Trade Commission Codes

The Federal Trade Commission on the other hand has for its purposes contracted the SIC codes. For the Quarterly Financial Report, it uses the two-digit SIC code on an enterprise basis. It has created its own code for the Line of Business Report, entitled *FTC Industry Category List*. This list includes 275 lines of business.

For its Corporate Patterns Report, the Federal Trade Commission has been using the five-digit Bureau of Census Code.

Internal Revenue Service Code

For compiling of statements of income, the Internal Revenue Service has created codes for principal business activity and principal products or services based on the ESIC. It includes 165 classifications.

Summary

Different agencies have developed their own codes as needed, usually basing them on the SIC or ESIC. Table 6-1, below, is a summary of the more significant codes that are used for lines of business.

PROCEDURES

The following is a brief summary of the procedures each of the major agencies mentioned above follows in classifying lines of business.

TABLE 6-1
Principal Lines of Business Codes

Code	Entity	Code digits	Approximate code size
SIC	Establishment	4	1000
ESIC	Enterprise	4	250
Census	Establishment	5	1300
IRS	Enterprise	4	165
FTC-QFR	Enterprise	2	24
FTC-LOB	Enterprise	4	275
FTC-CPR	Establishment	5	1300

Bureau of Census

Census assigns a code to each establishment of the reporting company. The code assigned is the code of the principal product line of the establishment, which may be a single physical location where manufacturing is performed. If a company operates in two or more distinct lines of business at the same location, a separate report is filed for each activity, each being considered a separate establishment. Most of the information requested is statistical and economic in nature and has to do more with production and shipments rather than with financial data. Most companies have very little difficulty complying with the requests of Census in their quinquennial report.

Annual Reports are condensed versions of the quinquennial report and just highlight some of the data that are published. Much of the information is operational, concerned with payroll, hours, quantities of materials used and materials produced, capital expenditures, quantity of electricity and fuels used, and the like.

The data reported by companies and kept by Census are treated as highly confidential. Each form carries the following notice: "Response to this inquiry is required by law (Title 13, U.S. Code). By the same law, your report to the Census Bureau is confidential. It may be seen by only sworn Census employees and may be used only for statistical purposes. The law also provides that copies retained in your files are immune from legal process." The 1972 Economic Census consisted of 20 volumes and included 683 reports covering the following categories:

- Retail trade
- Wholesale trade
- Selected service industries
- Construction industries
- Manufacturers
- Mineral industries
- Transportation

Internal Revenue Service

The Internal Revenue Service prepares a report—*Statistics of Income*— which results from information gathered from corporate tax returns. The corporate income tax return has a box in which the taxpayer is required to indicate an SIC classification. The tax-return instructions have a 1-page listing of the principal business activities based upon the SIC Code; using the list, the taxpayer must "enter the code of the specific industrial group from which the largest percentage of total receipts is derived." The list consists of 49 major industrial divisions which are further stratified into 165 minor divisions. The taxpayer is also required to "state the principal business activity and the principal products or services that account for the largest percentage of total receipts." With these two data, the IRS assigns the taxpayer to a single code, either that number indicated by the taxpayer, or another number from the activity information and other information available to it.

These data are aggregated and reported in a book of more than 300 pages. The information is considered of high quality because of the uniformity and the consistency required in tax-return reporting of each corporation from year to year. It has many uses both within and outside the government. There are two failings in this program: (1) the data are reported quite late, and (2) the data are seriously contaminated because an entire corporation, consolidation, or enterprise reports under one code. Still, the program is important for many uses.

As far as the taxpayer is concerned, the selection of an SIC code and the description of principal activities is a fairly simple matter, and many taxpayers give little thought to the importance of this selection for the stream of federal government statistics. Care should be taken in selecting an SIC code and in describing activities; any changes that may have occurred should be duly noted.

Federal Trade Commission— Quarterly Financial Reports

The Quarterly Financial Report (QFR) is probably the most significant reporting program within the federal government and has important impact upon published statistics. It is important because of its age (it was inaugurated in 1947) and because it is the only current information available. The data are usually published approximately 90 days after the end of the quarter in a volume of approximately 90 pages. The QFR publishes up-to-date aggregate statistics on the financial results and position of U.S. corporations. Each calendar quarter, based upon an extensive sample survey, the QFR presents estimated statements of income and retained earnings, balance sheets, and the latest financial and operating ratios for all manufacturing corporations and for mining and trade corporations. The main purpose of the QFR is to provide timely, accurate data on business and financial conditions for use by government and private-sector organizations and individuals. The report is prepared on an enterprise basis and takes only domestic operations into account. The sample is developed by stratifying the corporations in each industry and consists of two parts. The larger companies in each industry are permanent members of the sample, and smaller companies are rotated, each selected company being included in the sample for 8 quarters or 2 full years. The sample is approximately 17,000 corporations.

Forms NB are used for assigning respondent companies to one of 23 industries. These forms provide for reporting gross receipts on a percentage basis, segmenting the total domestic receipts to major product lines so that they add up to 100 percent. Based upon these data on the report form and other information, the reporting company is assigned to a single industry.

The assignments are basically into 10 nondurable manufacturing industries, 10 durable manufacturing industries, mining, retail trade, and wholesale trade. These industries are developed from the major two-digit SIC codes.

Quarterly earnings data and balance sheet data are submitted to the Federal Trade Commission on Form MG. In order to expedite the information, respondents are permitted to estimate the information in the reports that are filed. The explanatory comments state:

> Each corporation in the survey is required to provide a breakdown of gross receipts by source industry. These data are analyzed to determine in which industry or in which group the corporation will be classified. A reporting corporation is initially classified into the particular ESIC division which accounts for more gross receipts than any other ESIC division.
>
> To be in scope for the QFR, more gross receipts of the reporting corporation must be accounted for by either (not a combination of) ESIC Division B (Mining) or D (Manufacturing) or F (Wholesale Trade) or G (Retail Trade) and any other ESIC division.

A corporation assigned to the manufacturing division is normally classified further by the two-digit ESIC major group which accounts for more gross receipts than any other two-digit manufacturing group. In certain cases, the reporting corporation is classified further into the three-digit ESIC group which accounts for more gross receipts than any other three-digit ESIC group *within* the two-digit ESIC major group in which the reporting corporation is classified.

It should be noted that these procedures may lead to a conglomerate corporation being assigned to an industry group which accounts for only a small portion of its receipts.

In view of this sampling procedure and the assignment of a company to a single code, a considerable amount of contamination can occur in the statistics. However, in spite of the contamination and in spite of the estimates and errors that may occur because of the sampling procedures, these data and statistics as reported are considered an important factor in other government statistics for which they are used. Therefore, any company required to file Form NB should take some care in reporting the percentages of gross receipts according to the instructions and complying as closely as possible to the major ESIC three-digit codes. The FTC permits estimates.

LB Report

Because of the importance of the FTC Lines of Business Program and the complexity of the LB selection process, these topics are discussed separately in Chapter 7.

Corporate Patterns Report

The Federal Trade Commission contemplates preparing a Corporate Patterns Report (CPR) every 5 years to conform with the quinquennial Census of Manufacturers. The data obtained for 1972 and for the prior report, which was prepared for the year 1950, are quite similar to a portion of the data reported upon by Census. Accordingly, the FTC expects to use the five-digit Census Manufacturing Code and the two-digit SIC Code, which is the major group class for nonmanufacturers.

The CPR calls for almost an exact duplicate of the data furnished to Census, and it is appropriate to submit the same amounts filed with Census. This duplication is necessary because of the nature of the FTC publication program and the internal use the FTC makes of these data. Any data submitted to Census come under its very strict confidentiality rule, which does not permit their use by other than certified Census employees. Furthermore, the copy of the report retained by the respondent company also comes within the purview of these confidentiality rules. Since the

FTC desires to use these data to study the concentration of markets and major market areas so as to determine which industries could be candidates for antitrust investigation and to make appropriate allocations of FTC resources, it must duplicate these data, not having access to Census details. Since Census data are developed on an establishment basis, there is no extra activity required by the company other than to fill out the CPR form with the same data furnished to Census.

The Securities and Exchange Commission

The Securities and Exchange Commission (SEC) was created by the Securities Exchange Act of 1934 principally to regulate the security markets and securities issued by corporations to the public. It administers this act in several ways; its importance to segments of business is in providing for disclosure of financial data for investors and other interested parties dealing in corporate securities issued to the public.

Statistical Activities. The SEC was originally engaged in gathering statistics principally for use by other agencies, although this was not part of its principal function. During World War II, the Office of Price Administration had the responsibility for gathering financial information in order to enforce price control. After the War, the Bureau of the Budget assumed authority under the Federal Reports Act for continuing these activities.

It was recognized that there was an ongoing need for the collection and reporting of corporate financial information on a quarterly basis, and accordingly, the present Quarterly Financial Report (QFR) series was begun in 1947. The SEC collected data from those companies whose securities were publicly owned and registered with them, and the FTC collected data from nonregistered corporations. In 1971, the program was completely transferred to the FTC. As a result of this transfer, the SEC no longer has any responsibility, desire, or need to collect and aggregate either segments of business or lines of business data.

The principal role of the SEC through the years has been to set up required reporting procedures by which publicly owned companies provide appropriate data to investors, financial analysts, and the securities market.

In 1974, at the suggestion of the Acting Controller General, the FTC, the SEC, and other agencies together explored the possibility of coordinating or consolidating the lines of business data needs and data collected by all agencies. Meetings were held with the Chief Accountant of the SEC and others, and the following conclusion was reached:

> The SEC does not in a strict sense collect data except to the extent that the company's 10-K and other reports are filed in its library in addition to being made publicly available.

To coordinate the SEC and the FTC segmental-reporting requirements would be difficult because of the basic inconsistency between their approaches. The SEC allows companies to define segments as they choose subject to broad guidelines, whereas the heart of the FTC approach is to develop financial-performance data organized according to carefully defined industry categories or lines of business. Each approach has been devised to serve a different need, and, as stated previously, the SEC approach does not meet FTC information requirements.

Disclosure Requirements. To comply with its mandated responsibilities, the SEC require companies to register securities that they desire to issue and sell to the public. Different forms have been devised for different types of companies, but the most commonly used is Form S-1.

Prior to 1969, registrants were required under Item 9 of Form S-1 and all similar registration forms briefly to describe their business, indicating among other things their principal products produced and services rendered.

Early in 1969, a small group drawn from the SEC staff under the direction of Commissioner Francis M. Wheat issued a report entitled *Disclosure to Investors—A Re-Appraisal of Administrative Policies Under the 1933 and 1934 Acts*, (referred to as the *Wheat Report*).

The report deals essentially with registration requirements under the 1933 Act, with the principal exemptions from registration under that Act, and with reporting requirements under the 1934 Act. The report states:

> The Commission has recently proposed revisions to certain of its registration forms to provide investors with information as to the 'approximate contribution which various lines of business make to a company's profitability . . . ' The conferences held by the Study strongly substantiated the need for this additional information in the prospectus. Appropriate segment reporting is equally necessary on a periodic basis in the Study's opinion. In Chapter X, the Study recommends that annual reports on Form 10-K contain a breakdown of

sales and earnings similar to that ultimately specified by the Commission for 1933 Act Registration Forms.[1]

It wasn't until October 1970 that these requirements were extended to Annual Report Form 10-K covering periods ending on or after December 31, 1970.[2]

In January 1974, the SEC proposed to amend the proxy rules which were adopted in October 1974 when it issued a release entitled "Notice of Adoption of Amendments to Rule 14-a, 14-b, 14-c, and 14-c-7. Under the Securities Exchange Act of 1934 to improve the enclosure in and the dissemination of, annual reports to security holders and to improve the dissemination of annual reports on Form 10-K or 12-K filed with the Commission Under the Exchange Act."[3]

Coordination with the FASB

These changes in the SEC requirements were not created in a vacuum, nor were they the result of unilateral action by the SEC. There had been considerable discussion among industry, the financial fraternity, accountants, and independent auditors concerning fulfillment of the needs for more detailed information and disclosure of segments of a business.

One of the more important activities was that of the Financial Accounting Standards Board, which had been studying this subject since its inception in 1973, culminating in Financial Accounting Statement of Standards No. 14 which was issued in December 1976.

On May 10, 1977, the SEC issued Release No. 33-5826 (and others) pertaining to a proposed rule entitled *Industry and Homogeneous Geographic Segment Reporting*, in which the recommendation of the Advisory Committee on Corporate Disclosure is included as follows:

> At its February 1977 meeting, the Advisory Committee agreed to recommend that the Commission take action to (1) integrate the textual disclosure required in Commission forms with the segmental financial statement disclosures required by SFAS No. 14 and (2) require the inclusion of segmental financial statement disclosure in interim reports on Form 10-Q.

[1] Securities Exchange Act of 1934, Release 8650.

[2] Securities Exchange Act of 1934, Release 9000.

[3] Securities Exchange Act of 1934, Release 11079.

The Commission requested comments on the 76-page document to be submitted during August 1977.

Action was then taken by the SEC in issuing Release 33-5893 during January 1978 to conform its segment reporting requirement to those of the FASB for reports filed with the SEC for fiscal years beginning after December 15, 1976 as required by the FASB. This included Regulation S-K establishing the rules and procedures to be followed.

Subsequently, on March 3, 1978, the SEC issued Release 33-5910 containing interpretations, guidelines, and administrative determinations of the Commission's staff regarding the classification by registrants of their business into industry segments. On the same day, it issued Release 33-5911 amending Regulation S-K to clarify that registrants may present line of business data for fiscal years beginning before December 16, 1976 in lieu of industry segment information for those years provided such data were included in a document previously filed with the Commission. (See Chapter 12, *Recent Developments*, for further details.)

SUMMARY

All financial statements filed with the SEC for fiscal years beginning after December 31, 1976 must comply with FASB standards. The SEC requires auditors' opinions for financial statements. Financial statements must be in accordance with generally accepted accounting principles (GAAP). To be in accordance with GAAP, financial statements must comply with FASB standards (among others), therefore companies must comply with SFAS 14. Hence segmented disclosures must be included. This is confirmed by Release 33-5893.

Based upon a statistical study of a sample of 92 companies, evidence suggests that product-line revenue and profit disclosures together with industry sales projections published in various government sources provide significantly more accurate estimates of future total-entity sales and earnings than do procedures that rely totally on consolidated data.[4]

---

[4] Daniel W. Collins, "Predicting Earnings with Subentity Data," *Journal of Accounting Research*, Spring 1976.

CHAPTER 7

Federal Trade Commission Line of Business Report

INTRODUCTION

The Federal Trade Commission line of business program applies only to approximately 500 of the largest manufacturing companies operating in the United States. Although there is no indication of future plans in the present literature, it is entirely possible that after a few years of experience with this program and after ironing out the major problems that exist, the program may be extended to other companies.

Because the program is in such limited use at this time, this chapter will only briefly discuss the procedures for determining lines of business as required for the FTC report. Knowing the FTC's approach to the government's needs, companies required to file Form LB may be able to arrange their accounting affairs so as to comply with government requests with minimum effort. It should be considered that the LB program is the only existing government annual report that includes procedures for companies to develop lines of business data involving revenues, operating income, and balance sheet information.

When the FTC proposed its line of business program, it became quite evident that it was new, different, unique, and controversial, and that many problems remained to be solved. Yet, the program also had its good characteristics.

The program calls for a mixture of line of business data and segments of business data. It tries to mold accounting into a statistical pattern which is not always possible. The problem arises because it is difficult to complete the forms and expensive for industry to prepare them. The resulting data are theoretically of value, but factually the evidence suggests that their value is questionable because the data are not clean.

The first such form was FTC Form LB 1973, which 345 of the nation's largest manufacturing corporations were required to complete. Of these,

122 filed suit or intervened in suits to enjoin enforcement. The FTC filed action against 106 companies to enforce the filing of the LB reports. On April 21, 1976, the FTC announced that it would withdraw the orders served on the 117 companies who failed to file the 1973 LB forms. LB 1974 and LB 1975/1976 are quite similar, but considerably modified from the original 1973 form. Accordingly, this chapter will concern itself with the forms which will be applicable for the years 1975 and 1976. The Industry Category List for Form LB (1974) is included as Appendix 3.

PURPOSE

The general instructions state that the purpose of the LB report is to enable the FTC to publish aggregated financial data for manufacturing industries. In preparing financial data, each line of business in the company's LB reporting section (as defined) shall be viewed as if it were a separate operating company for which financial statements are prepared.

INSTRUCTIONS FOR COMPLETING AND FILING

The instructions accompanying the form are fairly complex, consisting of 17 pages of general instructions. Each of the five schedules (some of which have several parts) comprising the form also has specific instructions. Accompanying the instructions is a glossary of terms used consisting of 6 pages and 17 pages of an FTC *Industry Category List for FTC Form-1974*. Understanding these complicated instructions is one of the problems mentioned by companies involved.

A great deal of the data included in this form are not in the format normally aggregated by many business organizations. Accordingly, it is necessary to take the information developed by the company's management information systems and to reshuffle it in such a way as to meet the requirements of the various LB schedules.

It is a major accounting and/or statistical exercise for companies that for the purposes of management normally report many divisions, establishments, and organizational entities to meet the specifics of lines of business under the FTC category list. Few, if any, companies, distinguish lines of business in their accounts in a way that is compatible with the FTC definition of a line of business. In order to conform with the industry category list, most companies would have to go through special compilations, even if they had an excellent management information system. The instructions permit reasonable, well-informed estimates by knowledgeable company staff. Of course, each company must assemble data in this way so that there is sufficient uniformity in the data submitted to aggregate them in meaningful statistics. Perhaps this is the price that must be paid for gathering such data and statistics; but they do serve a useful purpose for the government and for the private sector.

Line of Business—Definition

Line of business is defined as a consolidation of all basic components of the LB Reporting Section which have the same primary activity. A *basic component* is defined as a part of a company which is used in forming the lines of business. Some examples are establishments, product lines or groups, organizational units, and profit centers. *Primary activity* is defined as the industry category from the Industry Category List which accounts for the largest percentage of net operating revenues. The term *primary activity* may be used in the context of the whole company or of a part of it, i.e., a basic component or LB. Schedule II provides 2 pages for reporting descriptive data for lines of business and criteria for selection of basic components.

Industry Category List

The Industry Category List lists 233 FTC codes of four digits. So that these codes cannot be confused with other codes, each code number has a decimal point between the second and third digit. This list is related to the 1972 SIC and to Bureau of Census codes. The three-digit and four-digit codes in some instances are shown on the list so that cross references can be made. This is helpful because the FTC uses two or more SIC code numbers to establish the Industry Category List.

LB Reporting Section

The Glossary includes rules for consolidation that apply when preparing this report. It provides for consolidating domestic operations generally in accordance with the requirements of the United States Internal Revenue Code with the exception that the following are not consolidated:

- Foreign entities, either corporate or noncorporate
- Foreign branch operations (whether incorporated or not)

- Domestic corporations primarily engaged in foreign operations

- Domestic corporations primarily engaged in banking, finance, or insurance (as described in major groups 60–63, and in group 672 of the Standard Industrial Classification Manual, 1972 edition)

Companies that are required to file Form LB have to prepare a separate consolidation worksheet or revise their consolidating procedures. In the consolidating workpaper, it is helpful to prepare a subconsolidation of the units in the LB Reporting Section, which are defined as the parts of the total reporting company consolidated in accordance with the LB rules. The other sections can then be separately consolidated and added to this total to accomplish the consolidated corporate financial statements in accordance with generally accepted accounting principles. The three separate units would be the foreign section, the domestic regulated section, and the finance section.

For the purposes of determining the LB Reporting Section, the subconsolidation must be further segmented if branches in foreign countries are included therein. These must be eliminated (although not for normal financial reporting purposes) as a separate step to arrive at the appropriate LB Reporting Section which becomes the control for the future steps in arriving at lines of business.

With a consolidating worksheet such as that described above, information is also readily available for reconciling the combined LB totals with SEC Form 10-K or the annual report of the company, whichever is appropriate, as reported in Schedule IV.

SELECTION OF THE BASIC COMPONENTS

Basic components are the parts of the company which are used in forming the lines of business. The instructions for forming them include a section called *Criteria for Selection of Basic Components* which may be referred to. The following material is a condensation of the principal steps discussed in those instructions.

1. Examples of components are:
    - Establishments

    - Product lines or product groups

- Organizational units

- Profit centers

Thus a component may be an establishment or a part of an establishment. For practical purposes, components selected should be the smallest units accounted for separately in the normal accounting procedures of the company.

2. Compute the average establishment specialization ratio, as follows:

$$\frac{\text{Total operating revenues—all primary products of the establishment}}{\text{Total operating revenues of the establishment.}}$$

3. Analyze the components by primary or secondary products according to the FTC Category List. In those instances where the component is the establishment, the resulting ratio is both the average establishment specialization ratio and the average component specialization ratio.

4. For those establishments that are further segmented into components, the specialization ratio for each component is computed in the same manner as that for the establishment.

5. The average component-specialization ratio must equal or be greater than the average establishment-specialization ratio of which it is a member.

6. If the criterion in point 5 is not met, the components for the establishment should be revised, either by combining two or more components, or by separating some primary component into two or more components. The first might result in taking some secondary products and combining them with primary products whereas the latter might result in developing some secondary product that would not be part of the primary products, and therefore either procedure may result in a change of the totals used for determining the component-specialization ratio. If the criterion cannot be met, the FTC suggests requesting an exception.

7. Each component should be easily identified by its primary activity, and components having the same primary activity

should be combined to form an LB. This is not done if establishments are used as components. A line of business therefore could be a single component or a combination of several components.

8. Each line of business of $10 million or more in net operating revenue must have an LB-specialization ratio of 85 percent. This is determined by the following fraction:

$$\frac{\text{Operating revenue of the largest industry category}}{\text{Total operating revenue for the line of business.}}$$
equal to or greater than 85 percent

If the 85-percent criterion is not met, further disaggregation is required. In other words, the line of business must be reduced by removing some of the product lines. If the specialization criterion cannot be satisfied for one or more LB's using the existing books of account supplemented with reasonable estimating techniques where appropriate, the problem should be discussed with the LB program staff of the FTC and an exception to the rule requested.

For the purposes of establishing specialization ratios, the values of shipments by establishment reported to the Census or values computed from such reports can be used.

VERTICALLY INTEGRATED OPERATIONS

Special treatment is given to certain vertically related operations. Vertically related upstream operations not specifically listed may be consolidated with intermediate stages through manufacturing and reported together in the industry category of the final manufacturing stage provided that more than half of the intermediate stage output is used in the final stage. If the intermediate stage is used in two or more final manufacturing stages, it may be vertically integrated into each of the related final stages.

Similar treatment can be applied to downstream operations if appropriate. Furthermore, lines of business with less than $10 million net operating revenues may be consolidated and reported as a single line of business.

When selecting components, it should be remembered that the report not only includes net operating revenues but also operating income reportable in Schedule III(A) and an analysis of certain assets. For the purposes of the above computations, net operating revenues represent products that are actually sold. Transfers between lines of business are separately reported in the schedule.

It is desirable to conform as closely as possible to those lines of business that add up or become parts of the same segments as reported under SFAS 14 or any other internal segmentation. This simplifies making estimates for the LB Reports and conforms with the data included in the 10-K or the annual report.

CHAPTER 8

Selecting Segments of a Business

INTRODUCTION

The need to select segments according to SFAS 14 offers management an ideal opportunity to reexamine its organization structure, management information system, and internal operations. These reviews can be a part of the selection process or a separate activity as discussed herein. The improvements that will result can readily offset the cost of compliance, improve decision making, and result in progress and profit.

For those companies reporting on FTC Forms LB, or those public companies registered with the SEC, suggestions are made for coordinating these requirements with segment reporting by taking these requirements into account during the selection process. There are two procedures for selecting segments of business or lines of business.

1. The procedure required by the Statement of Financial Accounting Standards No. 14 and also by the Securities and Exchange Commission. Both are closely related and are selected by management according to stipulated guidelines.

2. The procedure required in reports to government agencies such as the FTC, the Census, the IRS, and others. This procedure is based upon or modified from the Standard Industrial Classification Manual (SIC). It is used for selecting *lines* of business (often referred to as *segments of business* by various government agencies).

This chapter shall deal with the first procedure.

In studying the definition of *segments of a business* as distinguished from *lines* of a *business*, as generally used throughout this book, it should be recognized that *segments* of a business result from taking the enterprise as a whole and analyzing it, dissecting it, disaggregating it into its several pieces, and then aggregating the results into logical segments according to the guidelines in SFAS 14.

On the other hand, the procedures with respect to *lines* of business (LB), involve the synthesis of product lines in accordance with the various codes used or dictated by each of the government agencies. Selecting lines of business and selecting segments of business are reverse procedures. To select lines of business, a company must take the data for each code (SIC, ESIC, FTC categories or others) and add them together until they equal the total of the enterprise. Whereas selecting segments of a business is a disaggregating procedure, selecting lines of business is an aggregating procedure. To quote from the SFAS 14, paragraph 6: "The information required to be reported is a disaggregation of the consolidated financial information." Although there is no specific statement about aggregation in the FTC Line of Business Report, the tenor of the instructions includes such language as "reported in the aggregate for those lines of business in each of which the company has net operating revenues." For details, reference is made to the Line of Business Form.

THE FINANCIAL EXECUTIVES RESEARCH FOUNDATION STUDY

The Financial Executives Research Foundation instituted a study which was concluded in January 1968, and published their findings in "Financial Reporting by Diversified Company" by R. K. Mautz.

The study reported that the basis for selecting segments may be established according to any of the following sources or needs:

- The legal organization of the company or entity, principally, the parent company and its various subsidiaries

- The internal control structure, based on the company's organization charts and related to the areas of management authorization and responsibility

- Product lines according to the SIC or ESIC codes as established for internal use on groups of products resulting from the same production facilities

- Geographical lines represented by the locations of the various major facilities

- Markets of various natures, such as ultimate consumers, customers of the enterprise, processors of their products, or geographical regions

- Segmentation for internal aggregation for comparison with published statistics or for meeting the need of reporting to government agencies

- Accounting expediency (that is, to conform to the accounting structure rather than to meet the need for economists' analysis of the data)

- Similarity of broad industrial segments to the ESIC codes for ease in reporting to government agencies and to furnish a means of defining a company's internal reporting data

There are pros and cons to each of these, but in trying to decide which basis to use, certain other matters should be considered. It is not necessary to select a single one when a combination of several may be the best solution to the difficult problem of deciding how to segment a complex organization. Some of the problems to consider concern the ability to meet the requirements mentioned hereinafter.

HOW TO START

To arrive at segments that are meaningful both to readers of the financial report and, more importantly, to management users of the data developed, one should bear in mind the purpose of financial reporting for segments of a business during the selection procedure.[1] SFAS 14, paragraph 5 says:

> The purpose of the information required to be reported by this statement is to assist financial statement users in analyzing and understanding the enterprise's financial statements by permitting better assessment of the enterprise's past performance and future prospects . . . . Information prepared in conformity with this statement may be of limited usefulness for comparing the segment of one enterprise to the similar segment of another enterprise.

Although this refers specifically to the user of financial statements, the segmentation of data by product lines, departments, cost centers, or other organizational units has even greater use and value internally, to management at all levels. Aggregating or disaggregating these units will lead to segments combining many of the units that make up the business enterprise. Much can be learned about the activities of a company by studying the results of the various pieces that make up the whole.

[1] Reference is made to the flowchart (Appendix 4) in connection with this and subsequent chapters.

Paragraph 6 goes on to state: "Another important matter to consider is that the statement is a disaggregation of the consolidated financial information included in the enterprise's financial statements. The accounting principles underlying the disaggregated information should be the same accounting principles as those underlying the consolidated information except that most inter-segment transactions that are eliminated from the consolidated financial information are included in segment information."

Paragraph 8 notes a significant exception: "Transactions between a parent and its subsidiaries or between two subsidiaries are eliminated in preparing consolidated financial statements. In preparing the information reported by this statement, however, transactions between the segments of an enterprise shall be included in the segment information."

These comments suggest a further consideration. In most instances, the financial statements will be accompanied by an auditor's opinion; hence the auditor, in order to comply with generally accepted auditing standards, will have to examine how the segments were selected to ascertain that they were selected in accordance with SFAS 14 and that therefore the selection and accounting was consistent with the prior years. Valid change can be made in the segments as reported, however, provided there is a proper explanation in the footnotes of the financial statements if the change is considered material. The auditor should be consulted before implementing the changes.

SFAS 14 refers to the enterprise's existing profit center as the smallest unit of activity for which revenue and expense information is accumulated for internal planning and control purposes and designates it as a logical starting point for determining the enterprise's industrial reportable segments (paragraph 13). While this view is valid, profit centers are chosen and grow as an enterprise expands or changes in time to conform with its organizational structure or management procedures. Profit centers may have been established according to managerial responsibility rather than logical arrangements of product lines. The rationale for some profit centers may no longer exist for such management control purposes, or the rationale may have been lost through many changes that occurred through the years. The selection process for SFAS 14 creates an ideal opportunity to reassess, reevaluate, and reestablish profit centers in a more logical arrangement or to follow existing product lines and production flows. In other words, it might be worth the effort to start from base zero and develop profit centers more or less along the lines put forward in the instructions and selection process described in SFAS 14.

DEFINITIONS

Certain definitions are incorporated in SFAS 14 that are pertinent here. Incorporated in these definitions are some points that assist in the selection of segments. Paragraph 10 includes the more significant definitions that apply to the matter now at hand.

> *Industry Segment*—A component of an enterprise engaged in providing a product or service or a group of related products or services primarily to unaffiliated customers for a profit. By defining an industry segment in terms of products that are sold primarily to unaffiliated customers, this statement does not require the disaggregation of the vertically integrated operations of an enterprise.

Neither the statement nor FTC Form LB instructions define the term *vertically integrated operations*. However, R. K. Mautz, in an article in the Financial Executive, in July 1967, entitled "Identification of a Conglomerate Company," makes the following comment:

> Integration is typically discussed as vertical or horizontal. A vertically integrated company is one that is active in two or more successive and related operations directed towards serving the same market or markets. Thus, a company might extract a raw material, transport it to processing plants, process it sequentially through a number of operations, transfer it to a storage area, hold it, transport it to a marketing facility, and finally sell the product. Providing all the steps in this sequence are related to serving the same market and are closely tied in with one another, the company may be described as vertically integrated.[2]

This definition can readily be utilized for the purposes of determining whether a segment of a business is vertically integrated.

The meaning of the term *component* is not defined in SFAS 14; as it is used herein it differs from *component* as defined in FTC Form LB Report.

Further important definitions from paragraph 10 read as follows:

> • *Reportable Segment*—An industry segment, (or, in certain cases, a group of two or more related segments) for which information is required to be reported by this statement.

[2] "Identification of a Conglomerate Company," *Financial Executive*, July 1967. Reproduced as Appendix C of "Financial Reports of Diversified Companies."

- *Revenue*—The revenue of an industry segment includes revenue both from sales to unaffiliated customers (i.e., revenue from customers outside the enterprise as reported in the enterprise's income statement) and from inter-segment sales or transfers, if any, of products and services similar to those sold to unaffiliated customers.

- *Operating Profit or Loss*—The operating profit or loss of an industry segment is its revenue minus all operating expenses. As used herein, operating expenses include expenses that relate to both revenue from sales to unaffiliated customers and revenue from inter-segment sales or transfers; those operating expenses incurred by an enterprise that are not directly traceable to an industry segment shall be allocated on a reasonable basis among those industry segments for whose benefit the expenses were incurred

For other definitions, see the Glossary (Appendix 2) and also the Glossary of Terms Used accompanying FTC Form LB, which includes many terms in general use that the LB Form defines in a way that sometimes differs from common usage.

DETERMINING REPORTABLE SEGMENTS

Companies with reasonably sophisticated management information systems for many years have had segmented reporting for their operations for internal purposes. Management was motivated by its requirements for budgeting, reporting, and control of its activities and was not influenced by any external requirements other than such contract responsibilities as royalty payments, bonuses, and rentals measured by revenues or activities. Management may also have been influenced by the need for some degree of segmentation in order to make appropriate marketing decisions.

As previously stated, the FASB suggests that an enterprise's profits centers might be a logical starting point for determining the enterprise's industry segments. Another logical point that might have been mentioned would be a list of the various cost centers of an enterprise aggregated into appropriate reportable segments. However, for our purposes, it shall be assumed that the enterprise either has decided to start from base zero and review its entire operating structure to arrive at industry segments, or that prior to the issuance of SFAS 14, the amount of data aggregated by product lines or profit centers was so limited that it would be useless for determining segments.

According to SFAS 14, of the systems that have been developed for classifying business activities—such as the Standard Industrial Classification (SIC) and the Enterprise Standard Industrial Classification (ESIC)—none is suitable for use by itself to determine industry segments for the purposes of this statement. It also states that the determination of an enterprise's industry segments must depend to a considerable extent on the judgment of the management of the enterprise (paragraph 12).

In paragraph 11, three basic steps are suggested by which reportable segments can be determined:

> *a*. Identifying the individual products and services from which the enterprise derives its revenues,
>
> *b*. Grouping those products and services by industry lines into industry segments,
>
> *c*. Selecting those industry segments that are significant with respect to the enterprise as a whole.

Criteria

In subsequent paragraphs SFAS 14 refers to a number of criteria that must be met in the process of determining segments. (These should be considered throughout the three steps mentioned above and are listed below but defined and described further in the text.)

> • The *10 percent rule* requires that each segment shall represent 10 percent or more of the combined revenues or 10 percent or more of the amount of operating profit or operating loss or 10 percent of combined identifiable assets. These tests shall be applied separately for each fiscal year and a segment must satisfy one or more of the above tests. (Paragraph 15b)
>
> • The *75 percent test* which provides that the combined revenues from sales to unaffiliated customers of all reportable segments shall constitute at least 75 percent of the combined revenues from sales to unaffiliated customers of all industry segments. (Paragraph 17)
>
> • It is suggested that reportable segments should be limited to 10. (Paragraph 19)

- If an enterprise operates in a single industry or a dominant portion of an enterprise's operation may be in a single industry segment, the segmented reports as required by the statement need not apply, but the single industry shall be identified. An industry segment may be regarded as dominant if its revenue, operating profit or loss and identifiable asset each constitute more than 90 percent of the related combined totals for all industry segments, and no other industry segments meets any of the 10 percent tests. (Paragraph 20)

These items are merely guidelines and are not intended to prohibit a more detailed disaggregation if that is considered to be desirable.

It also is suggested that the several tests shall be evaluated from the standpoint of interperiod comparability before final determination of an enterprise's reportable segments is made. Although it is not stated, from the auditor's viewpoint interperiod consistency is also a matter of importance and should be considered.

Products and Services Identification

The first step in the segment selection process is the identification of the individual products and services of the enterprise. This can be done by divisions, plants, subsidiaries, or any other logical grouping that is presently used by the company. If a company is subject to reporting on the FTC Form LB, the products and services can be listed in accordance with the FTC Industry Category List. Other suggestions are to use the SIC or ESIC codes as applicable. If the enterprise is a member of a trade association that gathers statistics for the trade, the product lines used for these statistics may be desirable for use. Some industries submit data to the Bureau of Census for special aggregations and accordingly may consider using these. However, the products should be quite definite. For example, if a company makes men's clothing, it should designate its product as men's clothing, and not enter separate lines for coats, vests, and pants. The way in which the product is used or sold is a significant guide for identification. If a product is made principally for internal use, some judgment may be required since the end sale may be in one or more distinct products. For example, if a company makes small electrical motors that are used in the manufacture of household appliances, industrial tools, farming equipment, all of which are manufactured in its own plants, it may give consideration to designating the motors as a single product line with intersegment transfers. On the other hand, if these motors are only used within their plant for home appliances and small consumer garden tools, it might be desirable to combine the motors, the appliances, and the garden tools into a single segment. In other words, the judgment of management must enter into play in determining and identifying the individual products.

Grouping Products and Services

The next step in the process is to group the various products and services in some logical industry segments. Several factors should be considered in this step. A comparative study of the nature of the products, production processes, the market, and marketing methods may indicate appropriate groupings of the many products produced in a substantial enterprise. The findings could result in a logical development of cost centers or profit centers similar to those in existence, or they might suggest complete revision. In other words, consider whether the aggregation and segmentation process will result in a useful tool for management in planning, controlling, and reporting.

At this point it might be desirable to consider the smallest organizational unit useful to management for control purposes and for reporting revenues, costs, and profits. There are many considerations that might have a bearing on the resultant groups of product lines. A few such considerations follow; they are not necessarily listed in order of importance.

- How should the suggested segment be related to the enterprise's organization structure?

- How may the industry segment be managed, controlled, or reported upon?

- What is the extent of integration with other departments?

- What is its relationship to production, sales, or use with other departments?

- What is the extent of joint products or by-products produced?

- What is the amount of interdepartment transfer, or, more specifically, intersegment transfer of the output of the departments under consideration?

- What common facilities are shared by the several segments being considered?

- What is the geographic dispersion of the plants producing the products or of the markets and distribution facilities?

- How do the rates of profitability of the products compare? Different classes of products may have different profitability and it is wise to group those products whose profitability rates might be comparable.

- What degree of risk is involved in the manufacture, use and marketing of the product? High-risk items can often be warranted only by high profits, hence, the growth opportunity of such products should be considered.

- What are the trends of the several segments being considered? Perhaps products with comparable trends may be grouped; or, on the other hand, products whose trends are cyclical and therefore offset each other may be grouped to get more level trend reporting.

- What are the capital demands of the different product lines? Those products requiring little investment should not necessarily be grouped with products of high capital intensity since the yields must be different in each type for effective results.

Since many factors enter into determining industry segment, this review may disclose good opportunities for restructuring the organization of the enterprise. Organizations often grow like Little Topsy. They depend upon the existing circumstances when departments or divisions are created and upon the availability of management personnel. Product lines may have been grouped under a managerial decision that no longer is valid. If management has desired to make reorganization moves but has never found the opportunity to do so, SFAS 14 can be used as the reason for reassigning industries within a managerial group. The above list merely indicates some of the considerations that can influence reorganization and also serve the purpose of simplifying reporting segments of business and lines of business.

The 10 Percent Rule

After identifying the individual products and services and grouping these products and services into industry segments, the next step is to determine which industry segments are significant to an enterprise as a whole and therefore would be identified as reportable segments.

To be significant, an industry segment must satisfy one or more tests under the 10 percent rule (paragraph 15). The basic rules are as follows:

a The industry segment should have revenue which includes sales to unaffiliated customers and inter-segment sales or transfers that is 10% or more of the corresponding combined revenues of all of the enterprise's industry segments.

b The absolute amount of its operating profit or operating loss is 10% or more of the greater absolute amount of

i Combined operating profit of all industry segments operating at a profit, or

ii The combined operating loss of all industry segments that incurred an operating loss.

c The identifiable assets of the segment are 10% or more of the combined identifiable assets of all industry segments.

Exhibit 3 gives an illustration of how to apply SFAS 14, paragraph 15b. It shows the selection worksheet of a multisegment company. This fictitious company has more than 15 industry segments that seem at first glance to have sufficient revenues and operating profits or losses to be considered as reporting segments. Applying the above rule, we find that the aggregate of all profitable segments is $2,340,000. Ten percent of this would be $234,000, and therefore all the industry segments of $234,000 or more could be considered as reporting segments. This would eliminate segments A, F, G, and M.

Using the first part of the 10-percent rule pertaining to revenues, we would only select segments A, B, C, N, and O, all of which have $8 million or more of revenues, which represents more than 10 percent of the $80-million aggregate revenues of all segments.

The test for identifiable assets according to 15c is not included since it is readily understandable.

The 75 percent Rule

SFAS 14 provides that all of the reportable segments shall add up to represent a substantial portion of the enterprise's total operations. The combined revenues from sales to unaffiliated customers only of all reportable segments shall constitute at least 75 percent of the combined revenues from sales to all unaffiliated customers of all industry segments. Assuming that the revenues in Exhibit 3 are sales to unaffiliated customers and do not include intersegments transfers, we find that we require a total of $60 million of revenues for reporting segments. Accordingly, segment A which does not meet the operating-profit-or-loss test but does meet the revenue test, should be included among the reporting segments. This is quite obvious when it is noted that it has the largest amount of revenues of any segment. Including segment A, we do meet the 75-percent test.

Reportable Segments Limited to 10

SFAS 14 does not define the limit precisely, but the Board suggests that the number of industry segments that would be identified as reportable segments should not be above the practical limit 10. In Exhibit 3, reducing the number of segments to 10 or less without violating either the 75-percent rule or the 10-percent criterion requires combining several segments into a single reportable segment. Upon further study, we find that segments D, E, and F are related because these products are generally sold in similar markets, although produced in different establishments of the enterprise and by different means. The three are combined under an appropriate name as one segment.

We also find that H and I are produced in the same plant and therefore jointly use certain machinery, equipment, and other facilities, and accordingly it would be logical for reporting purposes to combine these two segments.

Segments J, K, and L are principally products used in the southern parts of the United States and are the responsibility of one vice president because of his knowledge of this territory. They also have certain other similarities that would enable management to justify combining them in the reporting as a single segment.

Segments N and O are combined because they are relatively new product lines and they are both high risk so that it is anticipated that the marketing of these two products jointly will result in a more even distribution of earnings between them.

Accordingly, after all this shuffling is done, the annual report of the Multisegment Company would include eight segments. However, for internal operating management and control, it would have 15 product lines, and even these 15 product lines may be further segmented by products for internal purposes.

The organization of these product lines follows certain grouping categories required by the Federal Trade Commission Form LB, making reporting easier.

It is suggested that the selection of segments be discussed with the independent auditor to determine the auditing standards that will be followed in examining the financial statements and the statement of segments of business to determine compliance with SFAS 14.

The above procedures are merely possible steps to follow in selecting reportable segments. They do not take into consideration one very significant point companies often make. It often is stated that the selection of segments be made in a manner that will not disclose certain data that would be useful to competitors. Perhaps in many instances the disclosure of these data is no more useful to one company than corresponding disclosures of their competitors. Though the subject of competition should not be ignored entirely, in most instances the danger can be minimized so as to get realistic segment reporting that is helpful to internal management at all levels as well as to external readers of the financial reports.

DOMINANT INDUSTRY

Under some circumstances a company can avoid reporting segments of a business externally if the activities of the enterprise are in a dominant industry. This is according to SFAS 14, paragraph 20, which states:

> An enterprise may operate in a single industry or a dominant portion of an enterprise's operations may be in single industry segments with the remaining portion in one or more industry segments. The Board has concluded that the disclosures required by paragraphs 22–30 of this statement need not be applied to a dominant industry segment except that the financial statements of an enterprise that operates predominantly or exclusively in a single industry shall identify that industry. An industry segment may be regarded as dominant if its revenue, operating profit and loss, and identifiable assets, each constitute more than 90% of related combined totals of all industry segments, and no other industry segments meet any of the 10% tests.

Initially this would appear to apply only to small companies; a study of the subject, however, may result in the conclusion that fairly substantial companies can meet this definition. Paragraph 10(a) states: "By defining an industry segment in terms of products and services that are sold primarily to unaffiliated customers, this statement does not require the disaggregation of vertically integrated operations to an enterprise". On the other hand, paragraph 101 states: "Broad categories such as manufacturing, wholesaling, retailing and consumer products are not per se indicative of the industries in which an enterprise operates and those terms should not be used without identification of a product or service describe an enterprise's industry segments".

In release 34-11,079, the SEC required public companies to report financial data on segments of business in their stockholders reports for fiscal years ending in 1976 and thereafter. The rules for selecting and reporting are somewhat similar to those required by SFAS 14, and accordingly, an indication can be observed of the manner in which companies may report in future periods.

An example is observed in Form 10-K of the Xerox Corporation, whose annual report shows total operating revenues of $4.403 billion. Form 10-K shows the company's business products for 1976 as $4.192 billion. Accordingly, all other segments in the aggregate would only amount to $201 million or less than 10 percent. In its description, it indicates principal business products including a broad line of xerographic copiers and duplicators and also a communicating electronic typing system, telecopier transceivers and facsimile devices, typewriters, products for use by engineering reproduction departments, and other products. It is not clear whether the products other than the xerographic copiers account for the $201 million or whether they are part of the company's business products. It would appear from the above disclosed information that business products are considered the dominant industry of Xerox.

Another example is International Business Machine Corporation with annual sales of $5.960 billion and rental and service revenues of $10.345 billion. Its annual report and its 10-K for 1976 state: "IBM's operations with minor exceptions are in the fields of information handling systems, equipment and services to solve increasingly complex problems."

IBM's 10-K lists the following products:

- Data processing machines and systems

- Electric typewriters

- Input word processing equipment

- Copiers

- Educational and testing materials
- Related supplies and services

A similar situation exists with major textile companies; they have used such broad terms as *apparel fabrics*, *textile home products*, and *industrial and other fabrics*. Again the question is posed whether this is sufficient segmentation to comply with the requirements of SFAS 14.

Whether this manner of reporting is consistent with the objectives of SFAS 14 is yet to be seen. The SEC has addressed itself to this subject in release 33-5910, as discussed in Chapter 12.

FOREIGN OPERATIONS

SFAS 14 does not amend the disclosure requirements of Accounting Research Bulletin 43, Chapter 12, "Foreign Operations and Foreign Exchange." However, in addition to the disclosures required, identification shall be made of both the industries and the geographical areas in which equity method investees operate (paragraph 7).

Industry segmentation on a worldwide basis is a desirable objective, but it may not always be practical. It should be implemented to the extent that it is feasible to do so. To the extent that it is impractical to disaggregate part or all of its foreign operations along industry lines, the enterprise shall disaggregate its domestic operations and its foreign operations for which disaggregation is practical and shall treat the aggregate of its foreign operation for which disaggregation is not practical as a single industry segment. When that segment qualifies as a reportable segment based upon the criteria described above, disclosure shall be made of the types of industry operations included in the foreign operations that have not been disaggregated (paragraph 14). In other words, it is pretty much up to management to determine whether or not it is appropriate, feasible, and practical to include its foreign operations in the various segments of domestic operations. In any event, the extent of its foreign operation must be disclosed. This requirement does not necessarily mean that each geographical area of activity must be disclosed. Management can combine all of foreign areas as if they constituted one industry. The disclosure shall be presented either in the aggregate or by geographic areas if the revenue generated by the enterprise's foreign operations from sales to unaffiliated customers is 10 percent of the consolidated revenues as reported in the enterprise's income statement or if the identifiable assets of the enterprise's foreign operations are 10 percent or more of consolidated total assets as reported in the enterprise's balance sheet (paragraph 32).

No single method of grouping into geographic areas the countries in which an enterprise operates can reflect all the differences among international business environments. Each enterprise shall group its foreign operations on the basis of the differences that are most important in the particular circumstances. Factors to be considered include proximity, economic affinity, similarities in business environments, and the nature, scale, and degree of interrelationship of the enterprise's operations in the various countries (paragraph 34). A geographic area shall be regarded as significant for the purposes of reporting if its revenue from sales to unaffiliated customers or its unidentifiable assets are 10 percent or more of the related consolidated amounts (paragraph 3).

MANAGEMENT INFORMATION SYSTEMS

The *management information system* developed by a company is for use by all levels of management. The *management system* (or, as it is sometimes called, *information system*), is an overall company-wide means of communication between various levels within the company. It involves many aspects of processing data so that information is furnished where needed at all levels of management for logical decision making. The data involved are not only from accounting. They include production data; quantification of personnel; material usage; inventory control; gas, electrical, and water use; and all the many bits and pieces of information that communicate from the lower levels of management to the top and also report results from the top level down to the operating management.

In developing segments for operational reporting, consideration must be given to the existing management information system as it is, how it has been used by the company, and the effectiveness of the entire system. The segmentation procedure should take full advantage of the existing management information system. On the other hand, it should not fractionize the company so as to impair the usefulness of the data and reports that have been developed and used for many years.

Management systems often reflect the organization chart and the flow of responsibility and authority. The information generated reflects managers' responsibility to carry out their duties and to report upon the results of their decisions, and it enables them to perform effectively; this is as true at the level of the supervising foreman as at that of the chief executive officer.

Management information systems in some respects are keyed in with accounting procedures, which are integral parts of the system. The accounting procedures develop the raw material that end up in the segment statements, and therefore they should be considered in developing the segments. However, a logical segment arrangement may call for a revamping of the management information system and a revision of accounting.

The study of a company's operations to meet the criteria for establishing segments according to SFAS 14 may be an opportunity to examine the company's organization structure and management information system including accounting procedures to determine whether they are in step with the times and still serve management's needs. The changes indicated by such a study and their implementation may be most rewarding.

COORDINATION WITH FTC FORM LB

For those companies that have been ordered to submit a completed Form LB to the FTC, a further complication arises. This form requires reporting lines of business in accordance with the Industry Category List for FTC Form LB which is based upon SIC and Census codes. This list includes about 275 lines of business.

Many enterprises do not maintain records in accordance with these details. Therefore, when reportable segments are determined it is advisable to recognize this further need.

The initial step in developing segments is the identification of individual products and services. Before grouping these products and services into industry segments, it is appropriate to identify products according to the FTC Industry Category List. This would enable the enterprise to disaggregate each industry segment as required for reporting to the FTC as more fully described in Chapter 6.

COORDINATION WITH THE SEC

The SEC has long been considering the need for segment disclosure to stockholders in the various forms filed with it. Initially, registration statements filed on Form S-1 or similar forms required a description of business including a statement of the principal products produced and services rendered, and the markets for and method of distribution of such products and services. In 1969, in its Securities Exchange Act of 1934 release 8650, the SEC required lines of business reporting in filings of registration statements. In October 1970, it extended such reporting requirements to the Annual Report on Form 10-K and similar reports.

It was not until the FASB issued SFAS 14 that the segmentation requirement was extended to all audited financial statements issued in accordance with GAAP.

On May 10, 1977, the SEC issued release 13525 under the 1934 Act, following up on its statement that it would reconsider its position when a statement was adopted by the FASB. This release includes a draft of the proposed rule conforming SEC to FASB. It solicited comments from interested parties, to be submitted on or before August 10, 1977. Based upon the comments received, on December 23, 1977, it issued release 14306 requiring compliance with SFAS 14 for all fiscal years ending after March 15, 1978.

The SEC was first to issue specific instructions for how to report upon segments; Form S-1 (also applicable to other registrations forms) contains the following:

> *Information as to lines of business.* If the registrant and its subsidiaries are engaged in more than one line of business, state, for each of the registrant's last five fiscal years, or for each fiscal year ending after December 31, 1976, or for each fiscal year the registrant has been engaged in business, whichever period is less, the approximate amount or percentage of (i) total sales and revenues, and (ii) income (or loss) before income taxes and extraordinary items, attributable to each line of business which during either of the last two fiscal years accounted for
>
> A. 10 per cent or more of the total of sales and revenues,
> B. 10 per cent or more of income before income taxes and extraordinary items computed without deduction or loss resulting from operations of any line of business, or
> C. a loss which equalled or exceeded 10 per cent of the amount of income specified in B above;
>
> provided that if total sales and revenues did not exceed $50,000,000 during either of the last two fiscal years, the percentages specified in A., B., and C. above shall be 15 percent, instead of 10 percent.
>
> If it is impracticable to state the contribution to income (or loss) before income taxes and extraordinary items for any line of business,

state the contribution thereof to the results of operations most closely approaching such income, together with a brief explanation of the reasons why it is not practicable to state the contribution to such income of loss.

Instructions:

1. If the number of lines of business for which information is required exceeds ten, the registrant may, at its option, furnish the required information only for the ten lines of business deemed most important to an understanding of the business. In such event, a statement to that effect shall be set forth.

2. In grouping products or services as lines of business, appropriate consideration shall be given to all relevant factors, including rates or profitability of operations, degrees of risk and opportunity for growth. The basis for grouping such products or services and any material changes between periods in such groupings shall be briefly described.

3. Where material amounts of products or services are transferred from one line of business to another, the receiving and transferring lines may be considered a single line of business for the purpose of reporting the operating results thereof.

4. If the method of pricing intra-company transfers of products or services or the method of allocation of common or corporate costs materially affects the reported contribution to income of a line of business, such methods and any material changed between periods in such method and the effect thereof shall be described briefly.

5. Information regarding sales or revenues or income (or loss) from different services in operations regulated by Federal, State or municipal authorities may be limited to those classes of products or services required by any uniform system of accounts prescribed by such authorities.

Information as to classes of products or services. State for each fiscal year specified in 1 above the amount of percentage of total sales and revenues contributed by each class of similar products or services which contributed 10% or more to total sales and revenues in either of the last two fiscal years, or 15% or more of total sales and revenues did not exceed $50,000,000 during either of the last two fiscal years.

The SEC requirements are quite similar to those of SFAS 14. What complies with the SEC for public companies would, in essence, also comply with SFAS 14.

OTHER CONSIDERATIONS

Transfer pricing methods also require consideration. This subject improperly treated can cause conflict between managements of different segments. It can also result in poor management decisions if not adequately studied and sound decisions are not made. Again, appropriate segment selection can reduce the problem but never eliminate it. This subject is discussed at length in Chapter 4.

Two major accounting considerations should not be overlooked when selecting segments. Allocation of common costs (manufacturing, factory overhead and burden, administrative and corporate expense) is an important factor in arriving at appropriate segments. Appropriate segment selection can reduce the problem but never eliminate it. This subject is discussed in Chapter 5.

SUMMARY

Selection of proper segments is not easy. It should be a team effort so that all involved members of the enterprise management are included. Once segments are properly determined, segment reporting can furnish management with a good tool, in addition to complying with accounting standards and government reporting.

CHAPTER 9

Reporting Requirements

INTRODUCTION

The benefits from accumulating data are directly related to reporting procedures and to the ability of the recipients of the reports to make meaningful decisions on the basis of the data reported. Provisions must also be made to ensure compliance with external reporting requirements. Hence it is helpful to have knowledge of the essential data required for completing any report. The following highlights reporting on segments of business and lines of business.

Reporting requirements can be discussed under two basic captions. Firstly, reporting of segments of a business, which, in essence, includes:

- Reports used internally for management purposes

- Reports sent to stockholders, principally the annual reports but also any other complete set of financial statements

- Reports required by the Securities and Exchange Commission which, in essence, follows the Financial Accounting Standards Board's SFAS 14.

Secondly, reporting required by several government agencies on lines of business used for analytical and statistical purposes and for reporting upon business.

It is not the purpose here to describe in any detail how each of the reports is to be completed. This chapter gives an overview of the more significant reports so that comparisons among them can be made. The reports vary from the simple requirements of selecting an SIC number to be entered on IRS tax forms to the very complex requirements of the FTC LB Form.

Instructions for reporting according to the FASB are included in SFAS 14. The FTC Form LB includes copies of the format and instructions.

THE PRIVATE SECTOR

Many well-managed companies, both small and large, public and private, have been using lines of business, segments of business, or product lines in the financial information reported for management purposes and for operations for many years. These internal reports vary greatly and their value depends upon the ability of management to use the data and the sophistication of reporting as developed by the controllers or accounting staff. Companies can be segmented by divisions, departments, markets, product lines, management responsibilities, or any combination of these. The reports vary from simple flash reports of revenues and estimated earnings to complete financial statements for each segment including statements of earnings, balance sheets, and statements of changes in financial position, as well as supplementary data. Some companies may merely require the profit or loss contribution of each segment. Others may report net profit of each segment before or after income taxes. Some companies may group their product lines to avoid the difficulty of allocating common costs and also to eliminate a great variety of complications for accounting for intersegment transfers. Each company and its management must decide what serves their purpose and create a reporting system accordingly.

Prior to SFAS 14, privately owned companies were not required to submit any segmented date in the annual financial reports audited by their CPA's. For fiscal years beginning after December 15, 1976, financial statements must conform with SFAS 14 so that the independent auditor can give an opinion that the financial statements are in accordance with generally accepted accounting principles (GAAP).

Recognizing the public concern about the burden compliance places on small or closely held enterprises, the recommendations of the report of the American Institute of Certified Public Accounts (AICPA) on "Generally Accepted Accounting Principles for Smaller and/or Closely-Held Business, and the recommendation of the Board's Screening Committee and Advisory Council," SFAS 21 was issued in April 1978 suspending the reporting of segment information by nonpublic enterprises (see Chapter 12, *Recent Developments*, for further details.)

PUBLIC COMPANIES

In recent years, at the suggestion of the SEC, the New York Stock Exchange, and the AICPA, many companies have been furnishing varying degrees of information concerning segments of business as supplementary data to the annual report to stockholders. In 1974, the SEC amended the proxy rules, thus requiring segmented information in the annual report although such information was not audited or covered by the auditor's opinion. The reporting requirements of the SEC are similar to those required by the SFAS 14.

REPORTING FORMAT

The minimum reporting format is included in SFAS 14 and is illustrated in its Exhibit B. It provides the information shown in Table 9-1 for each industry segment reported upon by the company:

TABLE 9-1
Industry Segment Report

Sales to unaffiliated customers	XXX
Intersegment sales	XXX
Total revenue	XXX
Operating profit	XXX
Identifiable assets	XXX
Consolidated information required is:	
Equity in net income of investee companies	XXX
General corporate expenses	XXX
Interest expenses	XXX
Total income from continuing operations before income taxes	XXX
Identifiable assets	XXX
Investments in net assets of investee companies	XXX
Corporate assets	XXX
Total assets	XXX

Similar information is required for foreign geographic areas. The requirement is described and a report illustration is included in Exhibit C of SFAS 14. This reporting is the least complex for segments of business and lines of business where full reporting is required. Exhibit 2, "Comparison of Lines of Business Profit and Loss—Schedule III(A) and IV(B) and Information About the Company's Operations in Different Industries (SFAS 14—Exhibit B)," shows the format for the Statement of Earnings in comparison with the information required by the more complex FTC Form LB.

LINES OF BUSINESS REPORTING REQUIRED
BY GOVERNMENT AGENCIES

The following comments pertain only to those agencies other than the SEC that require lines of business data on a regular basis.

INTERNAL REVENUE SERVICES

The Internal Revenue Service prepares Statistics of Income on an annual basis based upon data extracted and tabulated from corporate income tax returns. In order to get lines of business data from this material, taxpayers are required to insert an SIC number in a box provided therefor from a list that accompanies the instructions for the corporate tax returns. The data from all returns are aggregated by SIC code numbers and together with other statistics are published in an annual report, *Statistics of Income-197X—Corporate Income Tax Returns*. The data are considered important and used by many government agencies. Its present principal virtue is that the data are considered reliable because of the consistency of tax return data, although they are contaminated because the total amounts for each taxpayer are assigned to only one line of business although the taxpayer may have significant and important activities in other lines of business.

BUREAU OF CENSUS

Manufacturing companies are required to report to the Bureau of Census, which issues large amounts of statistical data from these reports. Each establishment (as defined) for all companies in the major sample is required to file Form MA 100 annually, from which this Annual Survey of Manufactures is prepared.

An establishment is defined as the single physical location where manufacturing is performed. If a company operates in two or more distinct lines of manufacturing at the same location, a separate report should be filed for each activity.

The form requires certain limited financial data and also a limited amount of statistical data. The financial data required are:

- Annual payroll
- Cost of materials consumed
- Inventories—end of year
- Depreciable assets gross at original cost at the end of the year
- Rental payments
- Capital expenditures
- Quantity and value of products shipped by product class

The statistical data required are:

- Number of employees
- Production hours worked
- Quantity of electricity used
- Purchased fuel

Every 5 years, selected companies are required to complete forms that are rather more detailed than Form MA 100. Each establishment will receive a form designed specifically for its particular line of business. The questions and data required are keyed to the factors that are significant in the operations of an establishment in a particular line of business according to approximately 10,000 product lines. In order to meet their requirements for data for each of the 1,300 product classes and 10,000 products, more than 300 different report forms have been designed for this quinquennial census.

The end result of this massive statistical exercise every 5 years is 20 volumes in which there are 683 separate reports on all phases of industry and commerce. Since the Bureau of Census requires a separate report for each establishment and each establishment represents one line of business, there is no significant burden upon industry in trying to segment their operations to meet the Census requirements. Furthermore, most companies can supply the kind of information requested very readily from their management information systems.

FEDERAL TRADE COMMISSION

The FTC has three programs requiring gathering of data by lines of business.

Corporate Patterns Report

The CPR began in 1950 but no accumulation of data has been made between its inception and 1975, when data were requested for the calendar year 1972. The FTC has proposed requesting this survey every 5 years, to coincide with the quinquennial Census of Manufactures of the Bureau of Census. The information requested by the FTC is similar to the financial information reported to Census. Any information reported to Census comes under very strict confidentiality rules whereby the data reported by any company cannot be seen by any but properly authorized Census employees. Since the FTC desires to use this data for some of its studies of the structure of markets and competitive conditions, it must have values of shipments by manufacturer's product class and by major product group classifications for each reporting company. Hence the need arises for this separate program, which to a great extent parallels the Annual Survey of Manufactures of the Bureau of Census.

Quarterly Financial Report (QFR)

The QFR publishes aggregate statistics on the financial results and position of domestic companies based upon an extensive sample survey made each calendar quarter. Companies are required to report estimated statements of income, retained earnings, balance sheet, and some related financial and operating ratios. The QFR is widely used in government and is the only timely reporting statistics of this nature available to statisticians, economists, and government agencies.

Two sets of forms are used in this program. Forms NB-1 for manufacturing corporations and NB-2 for other corporations are filed annually, and the data reported are used for assigning companies to a line of business when the quarterly reports are made. The corporation is required to report the gross receipts realized from the following categories:

- Products made, processed, or assembled by the company with its own facilities

- Products made, processed, or assembled for other companies by others from materials owned by the company

- Products bought and sold without further processing or assembling by the company

- All other sources of income

The amounts reported are the estimated percentage of gross receipts by line of business. Using these data, each member is a assigned to a specific industry classification so that quarterly reports can be published, prepared from reports filed by approximately 12,000 companies, and tabulated by major classifications.

Form MG must be filed quarterly by selected manufacturing corporations, and Form TR is required for nonmanufacturing corporations. Each of these requests a statement of income and retained earnings consisting of 19 line items starting with sales receipts and operating revenues for the quarter and ending with retained earnings at the end of the quarter. A balance sheet as of the end of the quarter is required consisting of 21 line items for assets and 17 line items for liabilities and stockholders' equity. The form for both of these is somewhat similar to the financial statements used for internal financial reporting purposes. An audit is not required and the data can be reported to the nearest thousand dollars. Reasonable estimates are permitted. No signature or certificate is required on the form that is filed.

Form LB

This form is required from about 500 of the largest manufacturing corporations. It is complex and calls for a considerable amount of information by 275 lines of business in accordance with an Industry Category List (Appendix 3), derived from SIC or Census codes.

The following are the statements of purpose as presented in Form FTC LB, and a summary of the schedules that must be completed:

Schedule I—Identification Data for Addressee Company and Subsidiaries. The purpose of this schedule is to obtain selected identification data for the addressee company and certain of its subsidiaries.

The first column is for information about the addressee company and other columns for each active domestic subsidiary or active domestic branch of each foreign subsidiary.

The data requested are principally for identification purposes and to evaluate adherence to the Rules for Consolidation.

Schedule II—Descriptive Data for Lines of Business. The purpose of this schedule is to identify the firm's lines of business and to gather selected descriptive data for each of them.

Schedule III—Financial and Statistical Data for Lines of Business. The purpose of this schedule is to collect selected items for financial and statistical information for each LB of the company's LB Reporting Section. Note the following characteristics about Schedule III:

- III(A)—Profit and Loss Summary (18 line items)
- III(B)—Assets (14 line items)
- III(C)—Supplementary Data (32 line items)

Schedule IV—Summary Reconciliations. The purpose of Schedule IV(A) is to provide a reconciliation of financial data reported in Schedule III for all lines of business (Column B) with related financial information for the LB Reporting Section as a whole (Column D) and with financial information which is published in the company's form 10-K submitted to the Securities and Exchange Commission or in the company's Annual Report to Shareholders (Column H).

It consists of 7 columns and 13 line items.

Schedule IV(B)—Explanation of Adjustments to Schedule IV(A). This schedule is the means for describing the adjustments in column C and column G of Schedule IV(A).

Column C pertains to LB adjustments and column G to consolidating adjustments.

Schedule V—Footnote Attachment. The purpose of this schedule is to accumulate in one location all information required to be reported in footnote format. Each footnote item in Schedule V is cross-referenced to other portions of the instructions where the requirements of the information are initially set forth.

Schedule V(A) provides for nontraceable expense or asset items and traceable expense or asset items.

Schedule V(B) provides for the reporting of the amount of transfers between the transferring LB and the receiving LB. It also provides for reporting nonattributable applied research and development according to LB.

Schedule V(C) provides for reporting the amount of basic research, the average establishment-specialization ratio, the average basic component specialization ratio and the inventory valuation method changes, wherever applicable.

Schedule V(D) provides for depreciation method changes, wherever applicable and transfer valuation method changes, wherever applicable.

Schedule V(E) provides for recording proprietory/ethical drug breakdown (which is a special bit of information requested) and reconciliation of Column D—LB Reporting Section of Schedule IV(A)—with the QFR report, a section for clarification of responses inconsistent with the instruction and details about companies combined under the optional method as described in the instructions for Schedule I.

The complexity of the report and the difficulty for some companies to meet its requirements has resulted in litigation (see Chapter 11).

Exhibit 2 compares the profit and loss data for each line of business that must be reported in for FTC LB with the segment of business data required by SFAS 14. No further explanation is necessary.

CHAPTER 10

Auditing

When the Financial Accounting Standards Board issued SFAS 14 on "Financial Reporting for Segments of a Business Enterprise," the statement became a part of generally accepted accounting principles (GAAP). Before issuing their opinion, auditors are required to establish that financial statements are in accordance with GAAP. It is not the auditor's responsibility to bring the financial statements into conformity with SFAS 14; this is the responsibility of the reporting entity which prepares the financial statements. Accordingly, the American Institute of Certified Public Accountants through the Auditing Standards Executive Committee (Aud-Sec) has studied the problem and, in December 1977, issued Statement of Auditing Standards (SAS) 21 on segment information[1]: Auditing standards are the guidelines established by the profession for examining and reporting upon financial statements.

This SAS is necessary because SFAS 14 is first effective upon financial statements for periods beginning after December 15, 1976, and, in most instances, would apply first to all calendar-year corporations whose audited statements are to be issued as of December 31, 1977.

Management is responsible for disclosure of segment information, and the auditor is responsible for determining whether appropriate disclosure has been made in accordance with SFAS 14. Hence it is desirable that management be aware of the auditor's standards and procedures as they relate to the auditor's examination of the financial statements in general and specifically the segment information.

AUDITING STANDARDS VERSUS AUDITING PROCEDURE

The auditing standard merely establishes guidelines for the auditor in examining and reporting on financial statements. Auditing procedures

[1] During March 1978, the Auditing Standards Division issued an Auditing Interpretation to conform with SFAS 21 suspending Reporting of Segment Information by Nonpublic Enterprises. (See Chapter 12, *Recent Developments*, for further details).

pertaining to SFAS 14 depend upon the circumstances within the CPA firm, the extent that auditing procedures already in existence would enable the CPA firm to come to a decision upon the fairness of the financial statements taken as a whole (including SFAS 14 information), and the firm's experience with the specific client involved. SAS 1 clearly states the differences between auditing standards and auditing procedures as follows:

> Auditing standards differ from auditing procedures in that "procedures" relate to acts to be performed, whereas "standards" deal with measures of the quality of performance of those acts and the objectives to be obtained by the use of the procedures undertaken. Auditing standards as distinct from auditing procedures concern themselves not only with the auditor's professional qualities but also with the judgment exercised by him in the performance of his examination and in his report. (Paragraph 150.01)

Auditing procedures involve a great number of techniques and methods used by the auditors in their examination of the financial statements.[2]

AUDITOR'S OBJECTIVES

In examining financial statements in accordance with generally accepted auditing standards (GAAS) auditors apply auditing procedures they believe to be appropriate in enabling them to express an opinion on the financial statements taken as a whole.

With knowledge of the auditors' requirements, management can establish records and information to enable the auditors to perform their services effectively and efficiently. In applying their audit procedures, the auditors will give recognition to:

- Materiality

- Consistency

- Compliance

- Reasonableness

- Disclosure

[2] For a comprehensive discussion of auditing procedures see *Working With the Public Accountant*, by Adolph G. Lurie, published by McGraw-Hill Book Company, 1977.

Throughout the SAS, reference is made that the auditor's opinion is on the financial statements taken as a whole and that the procedures to be established should give recognition to this approach. If a separate report is required on segment information, the auditor may find guidance in Statement on Auditing Standards 14 pertaining to special reports (paragraphs 10–13).

MATERIALITY

Materiality is an important concept that guides auditors in many decisions as to the extent of the auditing procedures to be applied. SAS 1, paragraph 150.04, states:

> The concept of materiality is inherent in the work of the independent auditor. There should be stronger grounds to sustain the independent auditor's opinion with respect to those items which are relatively more important and with respect to those in which the possibility of material error are greater than with respect to those of lesser importance or those in which the possibility of material error is remote.

The auditor considers this in determining the nature, timing, and extent of auditing procedures to be applied in the examination of financial statements. Materiality of segment information is evaluated primarily by relating the dollar magnitude of the information to the financial statements taken as a whole (paragraph 5). It is significant that the auditor should consider qualitative factors in evaluating whether a material matter relating to segment information is material to the financial statements taken as a whole even though judging it to be quantitatively immaterial with respect to those financial statements (paragraph 8).

STANDARD OF REPORTING

The second standard of reporting is:

> The [auditor's] report shall state whether such principles [GAAP] have been consistently observed in the current period in relation to the preceding period. (SAS 1, section 420)

The second standard requires consistency throughout the financial statements. According to the new auditing standard (paragraph 11), inconsistency in segment information may occur because of:

- A change in the bases of accounting for intersegment sales or transfers

- A change in the methods of allocating operating expenses among industry or geographic segments

- A change in the method of presenting a measure of profitability for some or all of the segments

- A change in accounting principle (as discussed in Accounting Principles Board Opinion 20, "Accounting Changes")

- A change requiring retroactive restatement (separately discussed in paragraph 12)

If the nature and effect of a change as mentioned above are not disclosed and, where applicable, the segment information is not retroactively restated with respect to the inconsistency, the opinion of the auditor should be modified because of the departure from generally accepted accounting principles (paragraph 13). Inconsistencies may not create any significant problem since the disclosures and the retroactive restatements with respect to segments would probably not have any material bearing upon the financial statements taken as a whole. However, it is suggested that the possible effect of any changes in respect to segment accounting and reporting on materiality and consistency be discussed with the auditor in advance.

COMPLIANCE

SAS 21 suggests applying specific procedures that pertain to compliance to segment information presented in the financial statements (paragraph 7). These are:

- Inquire of management concerning its methods determining segment information

- Evaluate the reasonableness of these methods in relation to the sections in SFAS 14 pertaining to determining reportable segments

- Inquire as to the bases of accounting for intersegment sales or transfers and make appropriate tests

- Test, to the extent considered necessary, intersegment sales or transfers for conformity with the bases of accounting disclosed

- Test the disaggregation of the entity's financial statements into the segment information, review the segment information analytically, and inquire concerning relationships and items that appear to be unusual

- Include in the analytical review (1) a comparison of the current year's segment information with that of the previous year and any related budgeted information for the current year, and (2) a consideration of the interrelationship of elements of the segment information that would be expected to conform to a predictable pattern based upon the entity's experience

- Inquire as to the methods of allocating common operating expenses and assets used jointly by two or more segments

- Evaluate whether such methods are reasonable and test the allocation to the extent considered necessary

- Determine whether the segment information has been presented consistently from period to period

- If segment information has not been presented consistently, determine whether the nature and effect of the inconsistency are disclosed, and, if applicable, whether the information has been retroactively restated

REASONABLENESS

During the review and examination of all the factors in the previously mentioned procedures, consideration should be given to the reasonableness of the methods and procedures followed by the reporting entity, not only in connection with the financial statements taken as a whole but with the disclosure factors in connection with the individual segments.

In the test for compliance and reasonableness, specific procedures should be established to test for the 10 per cent rule on revenues, the 10 per cent rule on operating profit or loss, and the 10 per cent rule on identifiable assets. Furthermore, a test of the 75 per cent rule of combined revenues should be established.

DISCLOSURE

SFAS 14 includes illustrations showing how the disclosures may be made. In the test for compliance, the method of disclosure and data to be disclosed should be examined to ascertain that they comply with the appropriate sections in SFAS 14. These disclosures can be entirely in the footnotes to the financial statements, or they may be on a separate schedule on segment information as an integral part of the financial statements.

AUDITOR'S REPORT

The standards of reporting apply to the auditor's report, sometimes referred to as the auditor's opinion. Bear in mind that the financial data as included in the financial statements are the reports of the entity. This section of SAS 1 relates to the auditor's report and opinion. Since the standard auditor's report states that the financial statements are in accordance with generally accepted accounting principles, the statements including the disclosure according to SFAS 14 must follow the disclosure requirements as mentioned in that statement.

The first standard of reporting is:

> The report shall state whether the financial statements are presented in accordance with generally accepted accounting principles. (*Section 410*)

Statements issued by the FASB are considered generally accepted accounting principles and are therefore included under this standard.

The second standard of reporting is:

> The report shall state whether such principles have been consistently observed in the current period in relation to the preceding period. (*Section 420*)

This has been previously discussed.

The third standard of reporting is:

> Informative disclosures in the financial statements are to be regarded as reasonably adequate unless otherwise stated in the report. (*Section 430*)

The fourth standard of reporting is:

> The report shall either contain an expression of opinion regarding the financial statements, taken as a whole or an assertation to the effect

that an opinion cannot be expressed. When an overall opinion cannot be expressed, the reason therefor should be stated. (*Section 510*)

The auditor's report need make no separate mention of SFAS 14 if there is compliance in the opinion of the auditor and if the information is disclosed in the notes to the financial statements. However, if a separate report on segment information is a part of the financial statements, then a special provision for identifying this statement and the opinion of the auditor is required. Accordingly, SAS 21 includes, in paragraphs 17 and 18, guidelines for reporting.

CONCLUSION

Since the determination of business segments depends largely upon the judgment of management, it would appear appropriate that the auditing tests and procedures should depend upon the judgment of the auditor. It is appropriate for management to determine what procedures and methods, in general terms, will be followed by the auditors in complying with the new SAS. With this information, management can establish internal controls and internal procedures in a manner that would enable auditors to readily satisfy themselves that the financial statements and the segment data are presented fairly in accordance with generally accepted accounting principles (including SFAS 14) applied consistently with the prior period.

CHAPTER 11

Litigation

INTRODUCTION

The litigation between a group of corporations and the FTC may not be of direct concern to most companies but the resolution of this complex court action can have lasting impact in the future upon compliance of all companies to requests for data from government agencies. These cases involve such issues as undue burden upon industry, the authority of the FTC, confidential treatment of data, accounting vs. economic data and reporting, and classification of segmented data. Hence it is worthwhile for management to be aware of these actions as they progressed through the courts, the decisions rendered, and the activities of the FTC after the court makes its final ruling.

Although the number of companies involved is small, the companies themselves are large in relation to those ordered to file LB reports and hold a significant position in the industrial world. This chapter therefore gives the background and status of this litigation.

Segment of business reporting as developed by the FASB and as required by SEC releases has not resulted in litigation although, in some instances, there have been comments critical of certain aspects of these programs.

When the FTC issued orders for the filing of LB forms in 1973, it set litigation in motion. Similarly, when it issued its order on the CPR program for data for the calendar year 1972 based upon a resolution of July 29, 1975, litigation was initiated.

LITIGATION SUMMARY—CORPORATION'S BRIEF

Much of the material that immediately follows consists of highlights of the case derived from the brief of appellants filed with the United States Court of Appeals and should be recognized as furnishing their side of the case.

An appeal, filed on October 4, 1977 in the United States Court of Appeals for the District of Columbia Circuit in re FTC Line of Business Report litigation (No. 77-1728) stated:

> At the same time it entered a final order and in the instant litigation, the court below, on July 15, 1977, also entered a Final Order and Judgment in a companion litigation involving a challenge to the legality of another Federal Trade Commission reporting program, the Corporate Patterns Report Program. In re FTC Corporate Patterns Report Program, D.D.C., Master File Misc. #76-0126. Because the two cases pose similar procedure and legal issues, they were given parallel treatment by the court below, though never consolidated. The corporate parties in the respective cases have noticed separate appeals, and have filed separate stay applications and briefs on appeal before this court, since the two cases, while related within the meaning of Rule 8(b) of the General Rules of this court, involve separate and distinct FTC reporting programs and since the emphasis on appeal in the two cases lies in different areas.

In a Memorandum Opinion and Order filed January 31, 1977, United States District Judge Thomas A. Flannery combined Master File 76-0126, the FTC Corporate Patterns litigation, and Master File 76-0127, FTC Line of Business Report litigation. These are very complex lawsuits involving tremendous volume of filings with the courts as well as other data and testimony. There are approximately 40 law firms representing more than 150 corporate entities involved.

In view of the parallel treatment by the lower courts and the rulings from the Court of Appeals, the following discussion related to the FTC Line of Business Report litigation will apply equally to the Corporate Patterns Report litigation.

SUMMARY HISTORY OF THE LITIGATION

On August 2, 1974, the FTC issued orders to approximately 345 corporations to file LB forms for 1973. Over 200 of these sought timely administrative relief against the FTC on January 3, 1975 in the District Court for the Southern District of New York (as a class action) and on January 21, 1975 in the District Court for the District of Delaware. Additional corporations either intervened in these actions or filed their own actions. The Delaware District Court ruled in favor of the corporate parties on all motions for preliminary injunctions to bar the FTC from seeking enforcement.

In February 1976, the Third Circuit, on an interlocutory appeal filed by the Commission, sustained the Delaware District Court on the question of preenforcement jurisdiction but reversed the lower court as to the grant of the preliminary injunctions.

In the New York cases, the FTC successfully opposed the corporate parties' class action motion. In April 1975, while actively seeking enforcement of its 1973 LB orders, the FTC proceeded to adopt certain technical revisions to the LB form for the 1974 reporting year.

After hearings and other appropriate activity, the second round of LB/special-report orders—seeking data for the 1974 reporting year—was served by the FTC in August 1975. Following the FTC's summary denial of motions to quash these orders in December 1975, the existing actions in Delaware and New York were supplemented to cover the 1974 LB orders as well. Then, however, the FTC decided to seek a change in forum. To achieve it, the FTC voluntarily withdrew its 1973 LB orders, dismissed its "American Standard" enforcement proceeding in New York, and, representing its "intention" to file an enforcement suit with regard to the 1974 LB orders in the District of Columbia (a forum with no prior involvement in the litigation), filed motions under 28 U.S.C. paragraph 1404(a), in both the New York and Delaware cases, to transfer the pending preenforcement actions in those districts to the Commission's newly selected forum.

On July 30, 1976, the lower court entered a pretrial order consolidating the preenforcement suits transferred from New York and Delaware with the enforcement proceedings instituted by the FTC in the District of Columbia. In an opinion and order entered on January 21, 1977, the lower court sustained its jurisdiction over the preenforcement suits on the authority of the Third Circuit Court of Appeals decision, finding final agency action reviewable under the Administrative Procedure Act (432F. Supp. at 287-89).

In an opinion and order entered on April 12, 1977, the lower court granted summary judgment against the corporate parties on their claim—twice sustained preliminarily by the Delaware District Court—that adoption of the LB program constituted rule-making subject to the requirements of APA (5 U.S.C. paragraph 553). As to the issue of undue burden, the court refused to assess whether the data sought bore a sufficient relationship to the program's purposes to justify the imposition of the cost of compliance involved, and granted permission for no more than five of the corporate parties to file affidavits detailing absolute compliance costs.

Following an evidentiary hearing subsequently called by the court, the court rendered its final opinion in the litigation on July 11, 1977, ruling against the corporate parties on all remaining issues (July 11, 1977, Slip Opinion).

The court ultimately ruled that the FTC had not acted arbitrarily or capriciously within the meaning of the APA and also granted summary judgment against all of the corporate parties on their respective individual claims of undue burden even though it permitted only 5 of the 150 plus corporate parties to submit evidence on the issue. Finally, the court ruled that the corporate parties' claim that LB data could be disaggregated in violation of the FTC confidentiality regulations was "premature" because the Commission assertedly had not as yet made its final decision to publish the data.

BASIC ISSUES OF THE APPEAL

The following is a summary of the basic issues raised by the corporate parties to the litigation.

The companies contend that the LB program is a "rule" within the meaning of the APA (5 U.S.C. paragraph 551[4]), and that the program and its implementing orders to file special reports, must be set aside as null and void in view of FTC's failure to conduct a rule-making procedure.

The companies maintain that, as a freestanding statistical endeavor, the LB program would be judicially reviewable as "agency action" under the APA's arbitrary and capricious standard even if the court held that the program does not constitute rule-making.

The court, moreover, improperly and summarily denied the corporate parties all opportunity to prove that LB data would be irrelevant, useless, and misleading for any purpose, refused to allow all but 5 of the more than 150 corporate parties an opportunity to present evidence on their respective compliance burdens and refused to assess the burden imposed in relation to the relevance of the data sought to be collected.

A distinct issue raised in this case concerns the propriety of the Controller General's clearance of the FTC's LB form under section 3512 of the Federal Reports Act, as amended. That statute requires that the Controller General determine whether the information sought is not already available from another source within the government, and that the agency's request for the data would impose not more than the minimum burden, and the report form is appropriate for collection of the information sought. The Controller General, however, refused to apply the appropriateness criterion in determining to approve the LB form, even though it found that the data to be collected by that form would be "unreliable at best and may be seriously misleading."

Confidentiality Issue

The corporate parties have raised a serious question concerning the adequacy of the confidentiality commitments made by the FTC in connection with the LB program, based on the mathematical disaggregation of published LB data aggregates. The lower court refused to consider this claim on the ground that the FTC has assertedly not yet made "a final decision to publish the data."

The Noncomparability Issue

Both the SEC and the FASB have designed their segment financial reporting requirements for the purpose of enhancing the ability of investors and others to evaluate on a year-to-year basis the overall performance of prospects of the reporting company. In regard to the comparison of the segment data of different companies, the FASB specifically stated as follows: "Inter-enterprise comparison of industry segments would require a fairly detailed prescription on the basis or bases of disaggregation to be followed by all enterprises, as well as specifications of the basis of accounting for inter-segment transfers and the methods of allocating common costs to two or more segments." The Board concluded that it is not appropriate to specify rules and procedures in that degree of detail.

On the other hand, the essential design premise of the FTC's LB program is that the LB data reported by different companies will be sufficiently comparable to permit their aggregation into totals for LB categories.

Accounting Profits Vs. Economic Profit

While the FTC has claimed that the profit concepts ought to be measured by the LB program "is that of economic profit rather than accounting profits", it has conceded that fundamental differences exist between the two. These differences are discussed elsewhere in this book.

LB Category Heterogeneity

The FTC has asserted that "of paramount importance in establishing the reporting categories is economic meaningfulness. The individual goods or services produced by the company segments which are included in the category should be perceived by buyers as close substitutes for each other. And buyers should view this set of goods or services as poor substitutes or not substitutes at all, for other goods and services."[1]

Yet, the demonstrable fact is that the vast majority of the LB categories are so heterogeneous that little if any use could reliably be made of aggregate financial figures published therefor.

It is very clearly stated in a letter of one of the corporate attorneys to Congressman Robert Eckhardt, Chairman of the Subcommittee on Consumer Protection and Finance, Committee on Interstate and Foreign Commerce, as follows:

> The classification basis for the LB program would result in undue burden and produce information lacking in relevance and meaningfulness. . . . Industry's objection has been based on the fact that companies do not generate or maintain accounting records on the basis of the SIC codes (a fact generally conceded by the FTC), and that to report accounting information on such a basis would require costly allocations and valuations of intra-firm transfers. In addition to the cost factor flowing from the SIC codes, these codes do not conform with the economic or anti-trust definition of a market—i.e., goods or services which purchasers view as substitutable.[1]

In the same letter, it is also stated that the principal issue in connection with the Corporate Patterns Report, in addition to those pertaining to many of the issues in connection with the FTC LB report, is as follows:

> [Various] government agencies have strongly opposed the CPR survey for precisely the same reason which industry opposes it, namely, that the survey would improperly impair the privileged status of the same data collected by the Census Bureau under pledge and statutory protection of confidentiality and immunity from legal process (13 U.S.C., paragraph 9).

LITIGATION SUMMARY—FTC'S BRIEF

Lines of Business Report

Much of the following material has been derived from the brief of the FTC filed with the United States Court of Appeals on November 17, 1977.

[1] August 1973 Statement of Purpose; March 1974 Staff Supporting Statement.

It should be recognized as furnishing their side of the case. Some portions might appear repetitive after what has gone before, but it is necessary to establish the FTC position on the more significant matters involved in this litigation.

In August 1975, the Commission issued orders to some 450 of the country's largest domestic manufacturing corporations, requiring them to file 1974 Form LB pursuant to its authority under section 6(b) of the FTC Act. This section provides the power to get information from those who can best give it and are most interested in doing so.

In its LB program the Commission is endeavoring to collect financial performance information (sales, costs, profits) from nearly 500 of the country's largest manufacturers with respect to specific industry categories, which are based largely on the SIC system developed by the Office of Management and Budget (OMB). The Commission contemplates aggregating the data from different companies for each category and publishing reports reflecting only the aggregated data. Under the confidentiality policies adopted by the FTC for the 1974 LB Reports, the FTC will not make public any company's LB Report or the data therein (nor use them for law enforcement purposes) and will not publish aggregated data if they can be disaggregated to disclose individual companies' data.

The Commission plans to use the published LB data to improve the efficiency and effectiveness of its antitrust enforcement activities. Investors, managers, editors, and scholars are also expected to be able to use the data to further the effectiveness of our competitive system.

The 1974 LB Form consists of four schedules. These have been described previously. Numerous reporting options are allowed, and well-informed estimates are permitted where information is not available in existing accounting records.

The LB program has received substantial support from Congress, which has indicated, by appropriating funds for the LB surveys and otherwise, that the data will be useful to the Congress and other agencies in formulating policy, as well as useful to the public in general.

The 1974 LB report was not, as the companies intimate, developed by the Commission in isolation, without solicitation or consideration of the views of the companies required to complete it. The Commission began developing an LB Form in 1970. During the next several years, proposed forms prepared by the staff were reviewed by the OMB pursuant to the Federal Reports Act of 1942. Congressional dissatisfaction with the OMB's handling of the LB Form, as well as other report forms of the Commission and other independent agencies, led Congress, in November 1973, to amend the Federal Reports Act to vest a reduced review authority in the General Accounting Office.

In April 1975, the Commission published in the Federal Register a notice of the proposed form, invited comments on the form and related materials, and directly solicited comments from a number of interested persons, including most of the companies involved in this litigation. A day-long hearing was held in May 1975.

The Commission has also issued orders to companies to file LB Reports for 1975 and 1976, but it made no decision on the LB program for 1977 and subsequent years. The Commission's staff is presently considering possible changes in the LB program based on experience with the program thus far and on recent actions taken by the FASB and Commission on Federal Paperwork.

As of November 1976, 270 reports have been filed. However, a large number of companies in the survey filed or intervened in new actions in New York or amended their complaints concerning the 1973 LB orders, while a smaller group of companies sued, intervened, or amended their complaints in Delaware.

When most of the deadlines for filing 1974 LB Reports had passed, so that the Commission was in a position to sue all delinquents in one proceeding, the Commission announced its intentions to do so and sought dismissal of the preenforcement actions in New York and Delaware or transfer of them to the court where the enforcement proceeding was instituted. The Commission also decided to withdraw the outstanding 1973 LB orders. The proceeding was filed in the District of Columbia, that being the only jurisdiction in which venue was plainly proper as to all companies.

All of the actions were assigned to Judge Flannery, who, on July 30, 1976, after considering the parties' proposals, entered an order establishing the procedures to be followed in disposing of this LB litigation.

A similar mass of preenforcement actions and enforcement proceeding concerning the Commission's Corporate Patterns Report was also assigned to Judge Flannery. Although the reports are entirely separate and distinct, the issues raised were similar, and the CPR and LB cases were generally litigated in tandem in the District Court. Pursuant to this and subsequent orders, the Commission sought summary judgment as to all issues and the company sought summary judgment as to most of the issues.

In its first opinion, the Court denied the companies' motion to dismiss the enforcement proceedings. In its second opinion, the Court granted the Commission's motion of summary judgment as to most of the issues, holding that the Commission has not engaged in lawmaking, that the Commission's orders were valid under the Federal Reports Act, and that the claims of certain companies that the Commission might improperly use the resulting data in the adjudicative proceedings in which they are parties did not affect the enforceability of the Commission's orders but could be raised in those proceedings. The Court permitted the companies to file five additional affidavits of their choice concerning the issuance of compliance burden. After a two-day hearing, the court issued its third opinion making findings of fact as to compliance burden and ruling in the Commission's favor in the remaining issues it addressed. On July 15, 1977, the court entered a final judgment, ordering all respondents in the Commission's enforcement proceedings to file their 1974 LB Reports within 150 days, subject to such extensions as the Commission might grant pursuant to its rules.

The companies have appealed from the District Court's final judgment insofar as the court, having rejected their claims, granted the Commission's petition of divorcement, dismissed the companies' preenforcement actions, and denied the motion to amend judgment.

Corporate Patterns Report

A separate brief was filed pertaining to those issues that only involve the CPR litigation. The following are highlights, in essence similar to the Lines of Business statement of that case, and derived from the brief of the FTC filed with the United States Court of Appeals on November 17, 1977. It should be recognized as furnishing their side of the case. Beginning in 1975, the Commission issued orders to approximately 1100 of the country's biggest domestic corporations requiring them to file CPR reports pursuant to its authority under section 6(b) of the FTC Act. In its CPR survey, the Commission is attempting primarily to develop a data bank concerning market structure and the nature of the activities of the 1000 largest domestic manufacturers and certain other companies.

At the heart of the CPR survey is Form CPR-1, which seeks information concerning the reporting companies' 1972 value of shipments from domestic manufacturing establishments in terms of product class codes developed by the Bureau of Census on the basis of more general SIC categories developed by the OMB. The form also requests from the reporting company information on establishment sales for domestic non-manufacturing activities, consolidated net sales, and total assets, as well as a listing of and information about major acquisitions and disposals since 1972. Best estimates are called for if records providing accurate answers are unavailable and where a question cannot be answered fully.

The Commission intends to use the data as a readily available source of information to facilitate antitrust enforcement, economic analysis, and policy planning. Data are sought for 1972 in order to permit the CPR data from individual companies to be used in conjunction with the aggregated data published by the Census based on the comprehensive census of manufacturers for 1972. The CPR survey has received substantial support from Congress, which has indicated that the data will be useful to Congress and other agencies in formulating policy, as well as to the public in general.

The Commission contemplates the possible publication of the individual company data but has made no decision to do so, except as it has determined that it will not, in any event, do so prior to 1978, when the data will be at least 5 years old.

The present CPR survey is essentially the same as one conducted by the Commission for 1950, in which many of the same companies or their predecessors were included.

The Commission conducted a pretest of the CPR Form using a small number of companies and, in December 1974, submitted it to the GAO for review pursuant to the Federal Reports Act. The GAO invited and received comments on the CPR Form from the public, including many of the companies, and from its own consultants; and it advised the Commission that the form was consistent with the Federal Reports Act.

The GAO did, however, comment on concerns expressed by the Bureau of Census and others about the relationship of the CPR survey to the activities of Census. As a result, supplementing communications with Census and the OBM that had occurred at the staff level both before and after submission of the CPR form to GAO, the members of the Commission conferred with representatives of Census and OMB in a public hearing in June 1975. Census indicated that it could provide aggregated data to the Commission through special tabulations, but was barred by statute from providing the Commission with individual company data which are an essential element of the CPR survey.

After considering the views expressed, on July 29, 1975 the Commission adopted a resolution authorizing the use of compulsory process in aid of the survey. Some 390 companies, including most of the companies involved in the litigation, eventually filed motions to quash the Commission's order. In late December 1975, the Commission denied the motions then pending in an extensive statement addressing the objections that were raised. The vast majority of the companies in the CPR survey, approximately 853, filed the reports. Nearly all of the other companies, however, declined to do so, thereby occassioning this litigation. Thereafter, the litigation basically followed the same pattern as the lines of business litigation.

COURT OF APPEALS RULING

On July 10, 1978, the United States Court of Appeals for the District of Columbia Circuit ruled as follows:

> The judgment of the District Court is affirmed. The corporate parties shall comply with the Line of Business and Corporate Patterns Report orders as issued by the Federal Trade Commission within 30 days of the date of this opinion.

UNITED STATES SUPREME COURT

This ruling was appealed to the United States Supreme Court. In November 1978 the court refused to review the case and let the lower court decision stand, upholding the FTC's right to obtain the LB and CPR data.

CHAPTER 12

Recent Developments

INTRODUCTION

After the Financial Accounting Standards Board (FASB) issued its Statement on Financial Accounting Standard 14 in December 1976, it began to receive questions and comments about the difficulties in meeting the requirements of this generally accepted accounting principle. As a result of its later consideration of the comments received, the FASB reexamined some of the areas that created complaints and has since amended SFAS 14 by issuing SFAS 21.

The AICPA Auditing Standards Executive Committee likewise issued its standard and an interpretation to comply with the actions of the FASB.

The Securities and Exchange Commission (SEC), after issuing its release of Regulation S-K, including the rule of compliance with SFAS 14, had discussions with some registrants concerning the appropriate segmentation of their businesses. On March 3, 1978, they issued releases 33-5910 and 33-5911 to clarify the reporting requirements of financial statements for fiscal years beginning before December 16, 1976, and to provide interpretations and guidelines regarding the classification of businesses into industry segments. These recent changes will be discussed in more detail in this chapter.

AMENDMENT TO SFAS 14 REGARDING INTERIM FINANCIAL STATEMENTS

During November 1977, the FASB issued SFAS 18, which amended SFAS 14 by eliminating paragraphs 4 and 73 of the original statement. Paragraph 4 says in part:

If an enterprise issues for an interim period a complete set of financial statements, . . . this Statement requires that the information referred to in Paragraph 3 be included in those interim financial statements.

The FASB had the subject of interim financial reporting on its technical agenda. It had reconsidered the question of whether segment information should be included in interim financial statements and had eliminated the requirement to report the information specified by SFAS 14 in interim-period financial statements pending completion of the interim financial-reporting project. In response to an exposure draft of this amendment issued on September 20, 1977, sixty-five letters were received, virtually all of which expressed agreement with the amendment. Accordingly, SFAS 18 was issued retroactive to the effective date of SFAS 14 eliminating this requirement.

SUSPENSION OF REPORTING SEGMENT INFORMATION BY NONPUBLIC ENTERPRISES

A Statement of Financial Accounting Standards was issued by the FASB for public comment during April 1978, entitled "Suspension of the Reporting of Earnings Per Share and Segment Information by Nonpublic Enterprises" (an amendment of APB Opinion 15 and FASB Statement 14). This statement addresses itself to two subjects, but we will only discuss that portion pertaining to segment information.

One of the complaints about SFAS 14 was that it applied to all enterprises regardless of size and regardless of whether their securities are publicly traded. The principal complaint was that the statement imposes an accounting burden upon smaller, privately owned, enterprises which do not issue financial statements either to their stockholders or the financial community except as required by their lenders such as commercial banks, insurance companies, and others. Paragraph 70 of the original statement stated:

The Board continues to believe that there are no fundamental differences in the types of decisions and decision-making processes of those who use financial statements of smaller or privately-held enterprises. Many small or privately-held enterprises operate in more than one industry or country or rely significantly on a single or a few major customers or export sales. Information of the type required to be disclosed by this statement is as important to users of the financial statements of those enterprises as it is to the users of financial statements of larger or publicly-held enterprises.

On the other hand, the Accounting Standards Division of the AICPA, in its study of the application of generally accepted accounting principles to smaller or closely held enterprises, issued a report in August 1976 which says, in part:

> The Financial Accounting Standards Board should develop criteria to distinguish disclosures that should be required by GAAP, which is applicable to the financial statements of all entities, from disclosures that merely provide additional or analytical data. (Some of these latter disclosures may, however, still be required in certain circumstances for certain types of entities.) The criteria should then be used in a formal review of disclosures presently considered to be required by GAAP and should also be considered by the Board in any new pronouncements.

This subject was considered by the Financial Accounting Standards Advisory Council and the FASB Screening Committee on Emerging Problems. Most of the members of the Advisory Council and the Screening Committee felt that segment information should be an optional disclosure for certain enterprises.

On February 23, 1978, the FASB added a major project to its agenda: To consider establishing guidelines for distinguishing between information that should be disclosed in financial statements and information that should be disclosed in financial reporting other than financial statements, and also distinguishing between information that all enterprises should be required to disclose and information that only certain designated types of enterprises should be required to disclose. Special attention will also be given to financial statements and financial reporting of small or closely held enterprises.

Recognizing public concern about the burden on small or closely held enterprises to comply with certain financial-statement disclosure requirements, the recommendation of the AICPA report on *Generally Accepted Accounting Principles for Smaller and/or Closely-Held Business*, and the recommendations of the members of the Board's Screening Committee on Emerging Problems and its Advisory Council, the FASB has concluded that with respect to nonpublic enterprises SFAS 14 should be immediately suspended pending completion of the project referred to above.

A "nonpublic enterprise" for this purpose is an enterprise whose debt or equity securities do *not* trade in a public market on either a foreign or domestic stock exchange or in the over-the-counter market (this includes securities quoted only locally or regionally). Comments were requested by March 29, 1978. There was no public hearing on this subject. In April 1978, SFAS 21 was issued and made retroactively effective for financial statements issued on or after December 16, 1976.

AUDITING INTERPRETATION

Statement on Auditing Standards 21 (Segment Information) requires that the independent auditor modify the opinion on financial statements if segment information is omitted. Since SFAS 14 required segment information on all audited financial statements, the elimination of this requirement for nonpublic enterprises requires a change or amendment to SAS 21. The Auditing Standards Division chose to solve this problem by the issuance of an interpretation which is in the form of questions and interpretations thereon. It states:

> Because the initial applicability of FASB Statement 14 to nonpublic companies may be suspended in the near future, auditors' reports that are qualified because those companies' financial statements do not disclose required segment information will be of reduced utility to users of those financial statements. Therefore, it is appropriate for the auditor to express an unqualified opinion on the financial statements of a nonpublic company that omits segment information if there is no other reason to modify his report. However, until a FASB statement suspending the application of FASB 14 to nonpublic companies becomes effective, the auditor should include an explanatory paragraph in his report that indicates that the "financial statements do not include segment information and the suspension of the applicability of FASB Statement 14 to nonpublic companies is being considered by the FASB."

The interpretation also includes the following example of an explanatory paragraph that may be used:

> The accompanying financial statements do not present segment information concerning the company's operations in different industries, its foreign operations and export sales, and its major customers as required by Statement 14 of the Financial Accounting Standards

Board. Suspension of the applicability of that statement to financial statements of nonpublic companies is presently being considered by the FASB.

The revision of generally accepted accounting standards was approved in April 1978, and the Auditing Standards Executive Committee issued an amendment to its Standard 21 to comply with this interpretation.

SECURITIES AND EXCHANGE COMMISSION SEGMENT RELEASES

The staff of the Securities and Exchange Commission have been having discussions with selected registrants concerning appropriate segment reporting. Release 33-5910, confirms that registrants are to comply with SFAS 14 while providing interpretations, guidelines, and administrative determinations by the SEC staff regarding the classification of businesses into industry segments under generally accepted accounting principles. The release requires that registrants set forth financial data for those industry segments which will most usefully assist investors in analyzing and understanding the business in question and will permit a better assessment of the business's past performance and future prospects. Companies which are determined not to have made acceptable industry segment disclosures generally will be required to amend their filings with the Commission and to communicate this additional information to shareholders in some appropriate manner. The release confirms that the classification by a corporation of its business into industry segments is a subjective task and depends on the judgment of management. It states that the provisions of SFAS 14 present a logical procedure for the classification of a business into industry segments. However, the terms *industry line* and *industry* are not defined in SFAS 14. As a result of the absence of such definitions, some persons have stated that the terms should be interpreted broadly. The Standard Industrial Classification Manual (SIC) defines industries by kinds of business and allows enterprises to be classified on a one-digit, two-digit, three-digit, or four-digit industry code, whichever is considered most appropriate. This suggests that *industry* may be used to include narrow as well as broad-base groupings of products and services. (See Chapter 6 on SIC codes.)

SFAS 14 does not state how narrowly the term *industry* should be interpreted. The only comment at this point is that broad categories (such as *manufacturing, wholesaling, retailing,* and *consumer products*) are not per se indicative of the industries which the registrant should report, and those terms should not be used without identification of a product or service to describe the industry segments. (The current releases refer to the criteria and the rules that are discussed more fully in Chapter 8, *Selecting Segments of a Business.*) The release comments further:

> Some persons have argued that industry segments be separate and distinct from each other and should be identified as such only if they can be sold without having an impact on the earnings of the corporation's other industry segments. The Staff believes that the "with or without" or "severability test" as it is known is not an appropriate test for the determination of segments. This test is not set forth in Statement 14 although it was recommended to the FASB in response to the Board's request for comments on the issue of segment reporting.

The release continues with discussions of acceptable segmentation for certain industries based upon discussions with registrants. The following are examples.

Electrical and Electronic Products

The comment concerning this industry is as follows:

> In the Staff's view, an industry segment identified as electrical and electronic products may be too imprecise or may include too many disparate products to be considered one industry segment. Companies in the electrical and the electronic products business are likely to be in more than one industry segment because the various products have different markets and are produced in different manufacturing facilities. In addition, the organizational structure of the companies with which the Staff met, suggested that top management recognize differences, significant for business purposes, between the products in each group with respect to market served, marketing methods utilized and the major production and facilities required.

Forest Products

Corporations in the forest products business argued that they were in one industry segment for a number of reasons, principally that their products are all produced with a common raw material. The Staff comments:

Despite cost allocation problems and the production interdependence, the Staff believes that companies in the forest products business may be in at least three industry segments: paper and paper products; building materials, e.g., lumber and plywood; and container and packaging products.

Chemicals

The Staff concur with a large chemical company that determined that its industry segments were the same as its lines of business, mainly:

- Chemical/metals
- Plastic/packaging
- Bioproducts/consumer products

Drugs

A company in the pharmaceutical industry argued that it was involved in a single industry because it produces three types of products in common facilities, involving the transfer of material amounts of products from one part of the business to another, but it was determined that the company's pharmaceutical, agricultural, and chemical operations should be reported as three separate industry segments. The company also argued that cost and asset allocation might have to be arbitrary if the pharmaceutical, agricultural, and chemical lines of business were further broken down. The Staff noted that the company's three types of products have different uses and are marketed through different means.

Property/Casualty Insurance

The question of reportable industry segments for insurance is being considered by companies in that field and by the accounting profession. It has been suggested that insurance companies have only one reportable industry segment. The Staff does not believe that all insurance products are sufficiently related to be grouped together as one industry segment. Many of the products do not have sufficiently similar rates of profitability, degree of risk, or opportunity for growth; moreover, they are generally offered to different types of customers, and involve different marketing methods.

The above examples give a broad understanding of how the SEC considers segmentation of businesses into industries. In each instance, the SEC viewpoint, differs from that of the businesses involved. The same is true of many other companies that may claim to be in a single dominant industry. Since those companies that will be required to comply with SFAS 14 are public companies and therefore will also be required to meet the SEC regulations, it is highly desirable for any enterprise to study the approach taken by other companies in similar fields in their annual reports and their Forms 10-K. It also might be appropriate to have prefiling discussions with the Staff of the SEC and obtain their views so as to eliminate any subsequent difficulties.

Of course, nonpublic companies, too, may find it useful for internal reporting and management purposes to establish business segment accounting for evaluating the various activities they are involved in, and the SEC guidelines may be useful for their purposes.

Release 33-5911 is a technical release for companies required to report 5 year segment data in filings with the SEC and reports to stockholders. These companies may present the line of business data for fiscal years beginning before December 16, 1976, in lieu of industry segment information for later years, provided such data were included in a document previously filed with the Commission.

During July 1978, the United States Court of Appeals affirmed the judgment of the District Court in favor of the Federal Trade Commission. The appellants subsequently appealed to the United States Supreme Court, where the appeal was denied in November 1978.

SUMMARY

It is quite evident that the current developments in business segment accounting and reporting have clarified the general concepts. A major step in the right direction has been the elimination of segment reporting in interim statements and by nonpublic enterprises. The interpretation and guidelines established by the SEC are most helpful to companies struggling with the determination of business segments.

These changes indicate that those who have justifiable complaints should voice them to the proper authority and that recognition is given to valid suggestions provided there is a sufficient number of communications in similar vein. As an object lesson, recent developments suggest that managements or professionals who feel strongly about a matter required under generally accepted accounting principles, auditing standards, or the SEC should make their feelings known.

An international accounting firm, Alexander Grant & Company, has frequently voiced its concern about the unfairness of applying the same generally accepted accounting principles to large public companies and small nonpublic companies. They expressed their views on October 17, 1977, in connection with the matters discussed in this chapter, in an open letter to the Financial Accounting Standards Board published in *The Wall Street Journal* which states:

Gentlemen:

We deeply regret being forced to communicate in this manner on an issue of professional accounting. However, we are genuinely concerned that you are not reacting to a serious problem. A recent exchange of correspondence between the AICPA and the FASB makes it clear to us that the present FASB does not intend to consider relief from onerous accounting and disclosure requirements for the thousands of smaller and/or closely-held businesses across this country.

In August, 1976, an AICPA Committee which one of our partners chairs made recommendations to the FASB on this subject. In Financial Accounting Standards No. 14 you stated that you neither accepted nor rejected the recommendations of the AICPA Committee but nonetheless you made the Standard on Segments of a Business Enterprise applicable to all businesses, regardless of size or ownership. This action by the FASB is most troubling since your Chairman had previously announced at an Advisory Council meeting that closely-held businesses would be exempt from the Standard.

In addressing yourself to considerations concerning size, you have stated that you believe "that there are no fundamental differences in the types of decisions and decision-making processes of those who use the financial statements of smaller or privately-held enterprises." We believe this statement will strike the owner/managers of such enterprises the same way it strikes us—incredible!

In your recent correspondence with the AICPA, you have suggested that a conference be held to discuss this matter "early in 1978." We believe this is merely a delaying tactic. The time for talk is past. We need action. We believe that the Board should (a) immediately appoint a broadly-based task force to prepare a discussion memorandum on this subject and (b) contemporaneously suspend the application of the Segment of a Business Enterprise Standard—and possibly other standards—to smaller and/or closely-held businesses.

We hope that others who read this letter may agree with us.

Very truly yours,

Alexander Grant & Company

CHAPTER 13

Past, Present, and Future

In order to try to evaluate what the future has in store in accounting and reporting for segments for business, one must first look at what has had the greatest impact on the present situation as it has developed over the years. The development has progressed along two fronts. The first was determined by the lines of business statistics needed, obtained, aggregated, and reported upon by government agencies. The second was determined by the needs of business and industry, initially in connection with their internal operations, and then, as companies became more complex, for external reporting as suggested by the Securities and Exchange Commission and then the New York Stock Exchange, and later made mandatory by the Financial Accounting Standards Board's issuance in December 1976 of a new Generally Accepted Accounting Principle in SFAS 14 on segment reporting.

These two fronts met and clashed as a result of the FTC order requiring some 500 companies to furnish segmented financial data in Form LB.

IN THE PAST

Government

The following is a brief tabulation of the major events that had an impact upon government requirements for lines of business statistics:

1902   The Bureau of Census was created to gather data about business.

1913   The Income Tax Law was passed creating a source for government data from income tax returns.

1914   The Federal Trade Commission Act was passed establishing an agency to maintain an overview of business activities.

1933 The Securities Act was passed providing for full and fair disclosure of the character of securities to prevent fraud in the sale thereof and for other purposes.

1934 Several government agencies were gathering statistics for their own purposes but without consistency. An interdepartmental conference was formed to examine the problem.

1939 During World War II, the Office of Price Administration and War Production Board found it necessary to gather statistics on product lines for pricing control, for management of government contract quotas, for establishing quotas for manufacture and sales of products, for establishing rationing quotas, and other purposes related to the war economy.

1940 The first edition of the Standard Industrial Classification Codes was published to create a classification system for business statistics by product lines.

1947 The Securities and Exchange Commission and the Federal Trade Commission jointly started a quarterly financial report on product lines.

1950 The Federal Trades Commission issued its first report on *Industrial Concentration and Product Diversification*, covering the 1000 largest manufacturing corporations (CPR).

1960 The Internal Revenue Service started reporting *Statistics of Income*, which includes a vast amount of data obtained from the corporate tax returns. This report later began to report business activity based upon the ESIC codes.

1960s Through internal diversification and mergers, business became more complex, and these years were referred to as the years of the conglomerate. The statistics that were available to the government were confused and clouded because of this great activity in diversification.

1963 The Enterprise Standard Industrial Classification manual was developed from the SIC codes for gathering enterprise statistics as distinguished from establishment statistics which were gathered from the SIC codes.

1968   The SEC first required a limited amount of information concerning the lines of business in registration statements. This was expanded in 1969. In 1974, the SEC amended proxy rules to require product line data.

1973   After studying the problem, the first Line of Business (LB) Report was sent to approximately 500 corporations.

1974   Litigation was started by approximately 200 companies in an endeavor to quash this program.

1977   Judgment was issued by the District Court in favor of the FTC. The corporations appealed. The Commission on Federal Paperwork issued its *Report on Segmented Financial Reporting*.

1978   The Court of Appeals ruled in favor of the FTC. The corporations appealed to the Supreme Court of the United States, which refused to review the ruling.

Private Sector

The first concern of business about product line information is lost in antiquity. When an enterprise had two or more products, it initially was concerned with the sales of these to determine where its revenue came from. As cost systems became more sophisticated, those companies with expanded product lines became interested in the contribution of the various products to the profit of the entire enterprise. It is not easy to pinpoint the impact of these various activities as to specific dates. However, a few dates do stand out.

1965–66   Subjects related to product lines first appeared in the volume of the Accountants Index.

1966   The Accounting Principles Board appointed a subcommittee to study disclosure by conglomerate corporations.

1966   A 2-day symposium was held at Tulane Graduate School of Business at which the subject was discussed at length and the proceedings later published.

1968 The National Association of Accountants published its first pamphlet on this subject entitled *External Reporting for Segments*.

1968 The Financial Executive Research Foundation published its volume resulting from a research project on *Financial Reporting by Diversified Companies*. This volume has become the most authoritative work on the subject.

1970 The SEC required public companies to include segment data in Annual Report 10-K.

1973 The Financial Accounting Standards Board was created and considered segment reporting as one of its initial projects.

1974 The SEC extended segment reporting to annual reports.

1974 Litigation started by companies against the Federal Trade Commission.

1976 The Financial Accounting Standards Board issued Statement on Financial Accounting 14 on Financial Reporting for Segments of a Business Enterprise.

1977 The Commission on Federal Paperwork issued its study entitled, *A Study of Segmented Financial Reporting* with certain very definite recommendations.

1978 Recognizing comments and requests from several sources, the FASB issued Statement of Financial Accounting Standard 21 suspending reporting of segment information by nonpublic enterprises.[1]

It is quite evident from the foregoing that the paths of government and the private sector in the development of segments of business and lines of business was not a smooth development towards accounting and reporting as the data were required.

[1] See Chapter 12, *Recent Developments*, for further details.

THE PRESENT

The Federal Trade Commission had been hampered because the data required on lines of business has not been forthcoming from almost 50 percent of those companies ordered to furnish data that are important in the overall program. It has received data from other companies but no report has been issued on the LB Report. On the other hand, it is continuing to issue quarterly financial data which have found many uses in spite of the errors and contamination in the data as disclosed in the report of the Commission on Federal Paperwork.

Now that the litigation has finally been settled in the Supreme Court, the FTC is no longer compelled to mark time in further developments of its lines of business schedules.

Companies have developed procedures to comply with the FASB statement so that their financial statements, including segment data, can be attested to by certified public accountants.

The FASB has amended SFAS 14, deferring the requirement of segment information in interim financial statements. The Board has on its agenda a major project entitled *Interim Financial Reporting*, and it is proposed that until this project is completed, the interim reporting of segments should be deferred.

The Financial Executives Institute has created the Committee on Government Liaison to study the government's business information requirements and ways in which business can cooperate with the government in these programs by improving the dialogue between the two sides. This committee came about because of the problems regarding the FTC's LB Report and the suggestions by the Commission on Federal Paperwork in relation to segment reporting.

The report and recommendations of the staff of the Commission on Federal Paperwork were approved by the Commission in May 1977. Through its various organizations, the private sector, too, has given its approval to the recommendations in this report. These recommendations are summarized as follows:

- Establish an interagency committee to develop improved and more compatible classification systems to meet the needs of government agencies.

- An advisory committee representing the FASB, industry, and interested consumer groups, should work to develop the least burdensome segments of business reporting system.

• The interagency committee should consider SFAS 14 or other relevant FASB statements in the development of new segments of business reporting systems.

• The FTC, FASB, industry, government, and other users should work together during all phases of the development of modifications of the LB program.

• Provide notice to and an opportunity for interested persons to comment with respect to any future nonminor changes in the program.

• The FTC should continue to assess the compliance burden imposed by its LB program in light of the value of the information requested.

• Future changes to the LB program should include guidelines concerning the type of data generally entitled to confidential treatment.

Limited action has been taken with respect to these recommendations. An organization meeting of the recommended interagency committee was held with representatives of industry and other interested organizations present. No specific steps have yet been taken.

FUTURE

The future with respect to segment reporting is not too clear. However, such requirements by the government and by the private sector are here to stay.

The government needs data and will continue to get it in a modified form. The interagency committee will probably become active after the litigation is over and the guidelines established by the courts with respect to the all-important lines of business reporting.

The Financial Accounting Standards Board will review SFAS 14 and issue interpretation and clarification statements and perhaps amendments.

Items to look for are the following:

- Interim reports will probably include some modified interseg-ment data. The financial community feels strongly that it needs segment data quarterly as well as annually to assess the operations of companies. However, this must wait until the full study of interim reports is completed.

- The guidelines for establishing segments from the FASB will probably be modified so that there can be a greater degree of uniformity to enable these classifications to be aggregated in a manner similar to the government's requirements.

- On the other hand, the government could modify its need to conform more closely to the records that will be normally maintained by industry. This probably will be the result of the interagency committee functioning together with private-sector organizations such as the Financial Executive Insti-tute, the FASB, the National Association of Accountants, and others.

- It would appear that there is a possibility of some abuse of the provision for reporting of companies with one dominant in-dustry. The FASB might establish a dollar amount not to be exceeded as the criterion for companies in a dominant indus-try. Segmentation may follow lines related to the SIC codes or a modification thereof that will come out of the inter-agency committee.

- After the users of financial statements have had experience with segment data in financial reports, suggestions will be made to modify the information in such a manner as to make these data more useful for analysis of the financial data. This probably will be accomplished through a joint arrangement between the financial community and major public com-panies through one of the business organizations.

- Those smaller companies that have not utilized segmentation data for management purposes will discover the value of such lines of business and segments of business information for management purposes. This will eliminate some of the objec-tions raised for complying with the data required by the government.

- Companies will discover the value of the information aggregated and reported upon by the government and use it for comparison with their own data in the management decision making processes. To some extent, the major companies do use these and have their in-house economists evaluate the data. However, there are misgivings concerning the accuracy of the data. When these economists find that the new programs will improve the data, they will make greater use of the vast amount of the information that will be available.

- Through the functioning of the interagency committee, a number of government agencies that now have their own segment reporting programs will join forces and jointly obtain the information that they need from one agency gathering data for several agency uses. This may be hard to come by but it is a move in the right direction. Perhaps some of them will use the Bureau of Census, which has the biggest capability to gather and report data and can furnish other agencies with what they need. The big problem is that the Bureau of Census cannot divulge the source of the information as to individual companies because of the legislated confidentially under which they must operate. However, when some of these data are prepared in such a form that others can use it, a tremendous saving can occur in government statistical gathering and reporting.

Segment reporting and lines of business reporting is required for so many purposes and can be useful in so many ways that it would seem appropriate for all segments of our society to get together and coordinate the creation, aggregation, segmentation, reporting, understanding, and using of these data for the good of all.

EXHIBITS

EXHIBIT 1
Comparison of FASB, SEC, and FTC Segment of Business or Line of Business Requirements

	Statement of Financial Accounting Standards No. 14	Security and Exchange Commission Releases No. 33-5826 and 34-13525	Federal Trade Commission Line of Business Form (LB75–76)
Purpose	To assist financial statement users in analyzing and understanding the enterprise's financial statements by permitting better assessment of the enterprise's past performance and future prospects.	To provide necessary information to investors and to minimize any consequent burden to registrants by making the various disclosure requirements more uniform, by (1) Providing an integrated disclosure form (2) Coordination of certain SEC line of business disclosure requirements of SFAS No. 14 (3) Improving segment disclosure for the benefit of investors (4) Codifying SEC staff position with respect to business related disclosure	To enable the FTC to publish aggregated financial data for manufacturing industries.
Who must comply	An enterprise whose debt or equity securities trade in a public market, on a foreign or domestic stock exchange or in the over-the-counter market, (including securities quoted only locally or regionally) or that is required to file financial statements with the SEC.	All corporations with publicly owned securities registered with the SEC.	Approximately 500 large manufacturing enterprises selected to file FTC form LB.

Description of business segment (FTC-Line of Business)	A component of an enterprise engaged in providing a product or service or a group of related products and services primarily to unaffiliated customers for a profit.	Same as SFAS No. 14	The consolidation of all basic components of the LB reporting section which have the same primary activity. A basic component is a part of a company used in forming lines of business, i.e. establishments, product lines or groups, organizational units, and profit centers. The LB reporting section is the parts of the Total Reporting Company consolidated in accordance with FTC rules, which excludes foreign entities, branches and operations, and certain financial type corporations. Primary activity is according to the FTC Industry Category list which accounts for the largest percentage of operating revenue.
Reporting frequency	Annually when an enterprise issues a complete set of financial statements in conformity with generally accepted accounting principles.	When the registrant is required to file Form S-K, Integreted Disclosure Form, in connection with filing of Forms S-1, S-7, S-8, 10 and 10-K.	Annually

EXHIBIT 1 *(Continued)*

	Statement of Financial Accounting Standards No. 14	Security and Exchange Commission Releases No. 33-5826 and 34-13525	Federal Trade Commission Line of Business Form (LB75-76)
Principal domestic information to be reported	Revenues	Same	Revenues
	Sales to unaffiliated customers		Sales to unaffiliated customers
	Intersegment transfers for each reportable segment		Transfers to foreign section
	Operating profit or loss for each reportable segment	Same	Transfers to Domestic Regulated Section
	Identifiable assets for each reportable segment	Same	Cost of operating revenue Gross margin
	Aggregate amount of depreciation depletion and amortization for each reportable segment	Same	Other expenses—traceable Contribution margin Other expenses—nontraceable
	Capital expenditures for each reportable segment	Same	Operating income Traceable gross plant etc.
	Net income from and investment in net assets of unconsolidated subsidiaries whose operations are vertically integrated for each reportable segment	Same	Traceable accumulated depreciation, depletion etc. Net property plant etc. Traceable inventories Traceable all other assets
	Disclosure of geographics areas vertical integrated equity method foreign investees.	Same	Total traceable assets Nontraceable assets in similar details as above Total assets
Export sales	Included in above whether or not there are reportable foreign operations.	Same	Same

If export sales from Home country is 10% or more of total revenues disclosure is required in the aggregate and geographic areas deemed appropriate.	Same	Not required
Foreign operations If revenues generated or identifiable assets are 10% or more, report same as domestic operations either in the aggregate or by geographic areas.	Same	Not reportable
Reconciliation with Consolidated Financial Statements The information for individual reportable segments and for foreign operations shall be reconciled to related amounts in the financial statements of the enterprise as a whole.	Same	A separate summary reconciliation statement is required reconciling the reportable data with the form 10-K or the annual report.
MISCELLANEOUS ITEMS REPORTABLE FOR EACH SEGMENT.		
Aggregate amount of depreciation, depletion and amortization expense.	Required	Required
Capital expenditures	Required	Not required
Equity in net income from and investment in net assets of unconsolidated subsidiaries and other equity method investees whose operations are vertically integrated.	Required	Not required

EXHIBIT 1 *(Continued)*

	Statement of Financial Accounting Standards No. 14	Security and Exchange Commission Releases No. 33-5826 and 34-13525	Federal Trade Commission Line of Business Form (LB75–76)
Effect on income of a change in accounting principle (APB No 20)	Required	Required	Not required
Major customer (10% or more)	Required	Required	Not required
Payrolls	Not required	Not required	Required
Materials used	Not required	Not required	Required
Applied research and development activities.	Not required	Not required	Required
Percentage of inventory valued according to LIFO, FIFO, average and other.	Not required	Not required	Required
Percentage of depreciation depletion and amortization according to straight-line, sum-of-the-years digits, double declining values, and other.	Not required	Not required	Required
Percentage of gross plant acquire 5 years, 5 to 10 years, 10 to 20 years over 20 years.	Not required	Not required	Required
Percentage of transfers valued at market, cost plus markup, cost, other.	Not required	Not required	Required

Segment selection method and criteria	Depends upon judgment of management.	Same	For LB reporting section only, separate into components (establishment, product lines, profit centers, etc.)
	Each segment 10% or more of combined revenues, or	Same except 15% or more of combined revenues if total revenues did not exceed $50,000,000	Analyze each component by primary and secondary products according to FTC industry category list. Compute average components. Specialization ratio which cannot exceed the average establishment specialization ratio. Revise components until criteria met. Combine components and primary products into LBs. Each line of business with $10,000,000 or more revenues must be at least 85% specialized (see instructions).
	Each segment 10% or more of greater of combined profit segments or combined loss segments, or	Same	
	Each segment 10% or more of combined identifiable assets.	Same	
	All reportable segments constitute at least 75% of combined revenues not more than 10 segments.		
Single or dominant industry	The disclosures required need not be applied to a dominant industry segment except that the enterprise shall identify that industry. An industry segment may be regarded as dominant if its revenue, operating profit and loss, and identifiable assets each constitute more than 90% of related combined totals and no other industry segment meets any of the 10% tests.	Same	No such provision

EXHIBIT 2
Comparison of Profit and Loss Report of Form LB with SFAS 14 Report

	Form LB		
	Sched. III (A) For each LOB	Sched. IV (A) Combined LB totals	Exhibit B SFAS No. 14
Revenues from outsiders	xxx		xxx
Transfers—Other LBs	xxx		xxx
Transfers—Foreign section	xxx		in above
Transfers—Domestic regulated section	xxx		in above
Total Net Operating Revenues and transfers	xxx	xxx	xxx
Cost of operating expenses	xxx	xxx	
Gross margin	xxx	xxx	
Other expenses—traceable			
Media advertising	xxx		
Other selling	xxx		
General and administrative	xxx		
Total traceable other expenses	xxx		
Contribution margin	xxx		
Other expenses—non traceable			
Media advertising	xxx		
Other selling	xxx		
General and administrative	xxx		
Total nontraceable other expense	xxx		
Other operating costs and expenses		xxx	
Operating income	xxx	xxx	xxx*
The following are not by lines of business or segments:			
Non operating income net of expense		xxx	
Interest expense		(xxx)	(xxx)
Equity in net income of unconsolidated company			xxx
General corporate expense			(xxx)
Income from continuing operations before income taxes and other items (forward)		xxx	xxx†

(Forward)	xxx					
Provision for income taxes	xxx					
Income from continuing operations before other items	xxx					
Discontinued operations net of taxes	xxx					
Income before other items	xxx					
Extraordinary items net of taxes	xxx					
Cumulative effect of accounting changes	xxx				in above	
Minority stockholders interest	xxx					
Net income	xxx					

* Does not include general corporate expense.

† Items other than discontinued operations are included.

EXHIBIT 3
Multisegment Company Segment Selection Worksheet
(In Thousands Dollars)

		Operating			Reporting Segments	
					Final	
Industry segment	Rev- enues	Profit	Loss	Rev- enues‡	Rev- enues	Profit (loss)
A	$13,000*	$ 100	$	$13,000	$13,000	$100
B	8,000*	500†		8,000	8,000	500
C	10,000*	400†		10,000	10,000	400
D	6,600		295†	6,000⎫		
E	2,000		600†	2,000⎬	11,000	(995)
F	3,000		100	3,000⎭		
G	7,000		105			
H	4,000	450†		4,000⎫		
I	3,000	540†		3,000⎭	7,000	990
J	2,000		240†	2,000⎫		
K	1,000		250†	1,000⎬	4,000	(750)
L	1,000		260†	1,000⎭		
M	3,000	115				
N	9,000*	235†		9,000⎫		
O	8,000*		280†	8,000⎭	17,000	(45)
Others					10,000	10
	$80,000	2,340	$2,130	$70,000	$80,000	$210
		2,130				
Net Operating Profit		$ 210				

* Para. 15a—10% or more of combined revenues A, B, C, N, and O.

† Para. 15b—10% or more of $2,130—B, C, D, E, H, I, J, K, L, N and O.

‡ Para. 17—75% of revenues—$60,000.

EXHIBIT 4
The Diversified Company
Diagram of Major Organization Units and Product Line Interrelationships

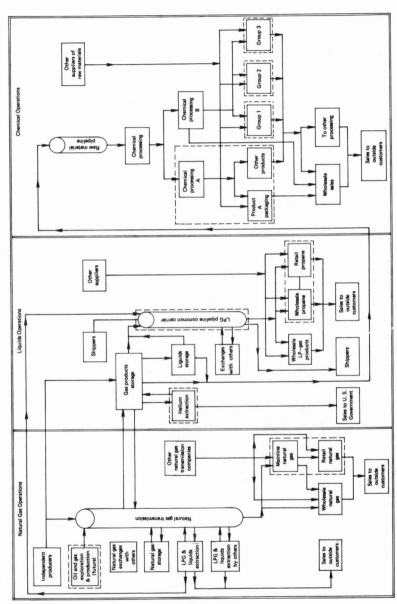

Courtesy of the Financial Executive Research Foundation, © 1966. Used with permission.

Major operating profit center—separated by double line
subsidiary profit centers—identified by broken line

EXHIBIT 5
XYZ Company
Interdependency of Operations

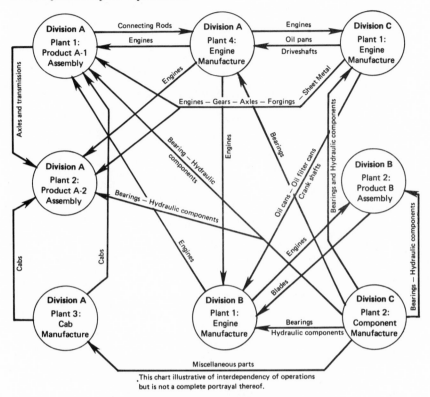

This chart illustrative of interdependency of operations but is not a complete portrayal thereof.

Courtesy of the Financial Executive Research Foundation, © 1968. Used with permission.

List of Appendixes

APPENDIX 1

Definitions of Abbreviations and Initials

APA   Administrative Procedure Act

CEA   Council of Economic Advisors

CFP   Commission on Federal Paperwork

CPR   Corporate Patterns Report

DOD   Department of Defense

ESIC   Enterprise Standard Industrial Classification

FASB   Financial Accounting Standards Board

GAO   General Accounting Office

LB   Line of Business

OMB   Office of Management and Budget

QFR   Quarterly Financial Report

SAS   Statement on Auditing Standards

SFAS   Statement of Financial Accounting Standard

SIC   Standard Industrial Classification

SOB   Segments of Business ·

SOI   Statistics of Income

Glossary

Definition of terms as used in this book.

Burden The economic and other costs of complying with a government request for information.

By-Product A secondary product of commercial value processed with goods or materials remaining or cast off from primary production.

Classes of Products Products grouped according to a scheme of classification which attempts to relate their common attributes.

Census An official count or enumeration, usually providing social, demographic, or economic information. With a capital C, *Census* refers to the Bureau of the Census, a part of the U.S. Department of Commerce.

Common Cost The cost of a good, service, or expense which is used for or attributable to the production of more than one product or to more than one organizational unit.

Contamination See Data Contamination

Co-product (Joint Products) Primary products necessarily produced by a given process. For example, producing mutton also gives wool.

Corporate Patterns Report A Federal Trade Commission data collection program dealing with the structure and composition of corporations.

Data Contamination The introduction of inaccurate, confusing, or misleading information which reduces its descriptive or analytic value. For example, reporting all of the data for a conglomerate under one line of business.

Disaggregation A rearrangement of accounting information included in the enterprise's consolidated financial statements so as to comply with Financial Reporting for Segments of a Business Enterprise.

Enterprise The sum of all establishments under common direct or indirect ownership or control.

Enterprise Standard Industrial Classification (ESIC) A data classification system developed by the Office of Management and Budget to identify and catagorize the commercial and economic activities of American businesses according to their operations or products.

Establishment An economic unit, generally at a single physical location, where business is conducted or where services or industrial operations are performed. For example, a factory, mill, store, hotel, movie theater, mine, farm, ranch, bank, railroad depot, airline terminal, sales office, warehouse, or central administrative office.

Federal Register A government document published each working day which contains agency regulations and other official information having general applicability and legal effect.

Horizontal Diversification (Integration) Companies or entities joining with others in the same or related businesses.

Individual Products As used in the Census of Manufactures, the finest level of detail for which output information is requested.

Line of Business Generally an economic or statistical term referring to a classification of business activities for the purposes of facilitating the collection, tabulation, presentation, and analysis of data relating to business and for promoting uniformity and comparability in the presentation of statistical data collected by various agencies of the United States government, state agencies, trade association, and private research organizations.

Management Information System A data system designed to provide information to management, usually including comprehensive information for analyzing, processing, and decision-making purposes by the entire organization.

Noninventoriable Common Costs Costs not included in manufacturing overhead or in inventory which can effect the total net income of the company, e.g. general and administrative expenses, institutional advertising, corporate office expense.

Operating Profit The accounting for a business segment consisting of revenue less all operating expenses including those allocated to segments on a reasonable basis as well as those directly traceable.

Profit (or Loss) The difference between revenue and expenses associated with the operation of a business concern. If expenses exceeded revenues, the difference is a loss rather than a profit.

Profit and Loss Contribution The accounting for a business segment consisting of revenue less only those operating expenses directly traceable to the segment.

Profit Center The smallest unit of an enterprise for which revenue and expense information is accumulated for internal planning and control purposes.

Quarterly Financial Report A comprehensive survey by the Federal Trade Commission every 3 months of approximately 12,000 business firms selected from manufacturing, trade, and mining industries.

Quinquennial   Happening once every 5 years.

Registered Corporation   A corporation whose securities are registered with the Securities and Exchange Commission.

Segment of Business   Generally, an accounting term referring to a component of an enterprise engaged in providing a product or service or a group of related products and services primarily to unaffiliated customers (i.e., customers outside the enterprise) for a profit. It is distinguished from *line of business,* which is an economic term identifying groups of homogenous products or processes.

Standard Industrial Classification (*SIC*)   The Standard Industrial Classification developed by the Office of Management and Budget for use in the classification of establishments by type of activity in which they are engaged.

Traceable   Those costs and assets which a company can directly attribute to a line of business or which can be assigned to a line of business by use of a reasonable allocation method.

Vertical Integration   The activity of an enterprise in two or more successive and related operations directed toward the production of a single or group of products for serving the same or similar markets.

Industry Category List for FTC Form LB (1974)

FTC Code	Description	Related 1972 SIC or Census Codes
	MANUFACTURING CATEGORIES:	
	Food and Kindred Products	
20.01	Meat packing, sausages and other prepared meat products	2011, 3
20.02	Poultry dressing, poultry and egg processing	2016, 7
20.03	Fluid Milk	2026
20.04	Dairy products exc. fluid Milk	202, x 2026
20.05	Canned specialties	2032
20.06	Frozen fruits, fruit juices, and vegetables	2037
20.07	Frozen specialties	2038
20.08	Canned, dried, dehydrated, and pickled fruits and vegetables including preserves, jams, jellies, dehydrated soup mixes, vegetable sauces and seasoning, and salad dressings	2033, 4, 5
20.09	Cereal breakfast foods	2043
20.10	Dog, cat, and other pet food	2047
20.11	Prepared feeds and feed ingredients for animals and fowls, nec.	2048
20.12	Flour and other grain mill products, rice milling, blended and prepared flour	2041, 4, 5
20.13	Wet corn milling	2046
20.14	Bread, cake, and related products	2051
20.15	Cookies and crackers	2052
20.16	Cane sugar	2061, 2
20.17	Beet sugar	2063
20.18	Confectionery products	2065
20.19	Chocolate and cocoa products	2066
20.20	Chewing gum	2067

A P P E N D I X 3 *(Continued)*

FTC Code	Description	Related 1972 SIC or Census Codes
20.21	Fats and oils	207
20.22	Malt beverages	2082
20.23	Malt	2083
20.24	Wines, brandy, and brandy spirits	2084
20.25	Distilled liquor	2085
20.26	Bottled and canned soft drinks	2086
20.27	Flavoring extracts and syrups, nec.	2087
20.28	Roasted coffee	2095
20.29	Misc. foods and kindred products, exc. roasted coffee	209, x 2095
	Tobacco Manufacturing	
21.01	Cigarettes	211
21.02	Cigars	212
21.03	Chewing and smoking tobacco	213
21.04	Tobacco stemming and redrying	214
	Textile Mill Products	
22.01	Weaving mills—cotton, synthetics, and silk	221, 222
22.02	Weaving and finishing mills, wool	223
22.03	Narrow fabric mills	224
22.04	Hosiery	2251, 2
22.05	Knit outerwear mills	2253
22.06	Knit underwear mills	2254
22.07	Knitting mills, nec., including circular and warp knit fabric mills	2257, 8, 9
22.08	Textile finishing, except wool and knit goods	226
22.09	Floor covering mills	227
22.10	Yarn and thread mills	228
22.11	Tire cord and fabric	2296
22.12	Misc. textile goods, exc. tire cord and fabric	229, x 2296
	Apparel and Other Fabric Products	

A P P E N D I X 3 (*Continued*)

FTC Code	Description	Related 1972 SIC or Census Codes
23.01	Men's and boys' suits and coats	231
23.02	Men's and boys' furnishings	232
23.03	Women's and misses' outerwear	233
23.04	Women's and children's undergarments	234
23.05	Children's outerwear	236
23.06	Misc. apparel and accessories, including hats, caps, and millinery and fur goods	235, 237, 238
23.07	Misc. fabricated textile products	239
	Lumber and Wood Products Except Furniture	
24.01	Logging camps and logging contractors	241
24.02	Sawmills and planing mills	242
24.03	Millwork, plywood and structural members	243
24.04	Wood buildings and mobile homes	245
24.05	Misc. wood products, including wood containers	244, 249
	Furniture and Fixtures	
25.01	Mattresses and bedsprings	2515
25.02	Household furniture, exc. mattresses and bedsprings	251, x 2515
25.03	Office furniture	252
25.04	Public building and related furniture	253
25.05	Partitions and fixtures	254
25.06	Misc. furniture and fixtures	259
	Paper and Allied Products	
26.01	Pulp mills	261
26.02	Paper mills, except building paper	262
26.03	Paperboard mills	263
26.04	Paper coating and glazing	2641
26.05	Envelopes	2642
26.06	Bags, exc. textile bags	2643

FTC Code	Description	Related 1972 SIC or Census Codes
26.07	Sanitary paper products	2647
26.08	Stationery, tablets, and related products	2648
26.09	Converted paper and paperboard products, nec., including die-cut paper, paperboard, and cardboard, and pressed and molded pulp goods	2645, 6, 9
26.10	Paperboard containers and boxes	265
26.11	Building paper and board mills	266
	Printing, Publishing and Allied Industries	
27.01	Newspapers	271
27.02	Periodicals	272
27.03	Books	273
27.04	Misc. publishing	274
27.05	Commercial printing	275
27.06	Manifold business forms	276
27.07	Greeting card publishing	277
27.08	Blankbooks and bookbinding	278
27.09	Printing trade services	279
	Chemicals and Allied Products	
28.01	Industrial gases	2813
28.02	Inorganic pigments	2816
28.03	Industrial inorganic chemicals, exc. industrial gases and inorganic pigments	2812, 2819
28.04	Plastics materials and resins	2821
28.05	Synthetic rubber	2822
28.06	Organic fibers	2823, 4
28.07	Drugs, ethical	pt. 283
28.08	Drugs, proprietary	pt. 283
28.09	Perfumes, cosmetics, and other toilet preparations	2844
28.10	Soap and other cleaning preparations	284, x 2844

FTC Code	Description	Related 1972 SIC or Census Codes
28.11	Paints and allied products	285
28.12	Gum and wood chemicals	2861
28.13	Industrial organic chemicals, exc. gum and wood chemicals	2865, 9
28.14	Fertilizers	2873, 4, 5
28.15	Pesticides and agricultural chemicals, nec.	2879
28.16	Explosives	2892
28.17	Misc. chemical products, exc. explosives	289, x 2892
	Petroleum Refining and Related Industries	
29.01	Petroleum refining	291
29.02	Paving and roofing materials	295
29.03	Misc. petroleum and coal products	299
	Rubber and Miscellaneous Plastics Products	
30.01	Tires and inner tubes	301
30.02	Rubber and plastics footwear	302
30.03	Reclaimed rubber	303
30.04	Rubber and plastics hose and belting	304
30.05	Fabricated rubber products, nec.	306
30.06	Misc. plastics products	307
	Leather and Leather Products	
31.01	Leather tanning and finishing	311
31.02	Footwear, except rubber; and boot and shoe cut stock and findings	313, 314
31.03	Luggage	316
31.04	Leather goods, nec., including leather gloves and mittens, and handbags and personal leather goods	315, 317, 319
	Stone, Clay, Glass, and Concrete Products	
32.01	Flat glass	321
32.02	Glass containers	3221
32.03	Pressed and blown glass, nec.	3229

FTC Code	Description	Related 1972 SIC or Census Codes
32.04	Products of purchased glass	323
32.05	Cement, hydraulic	324
32.06	Structural clay products	325
32.07	Vitreous plumbing fixtures	3261
32.08	Porcelain electrical supplies	3264
32.09	Pottery and related products, exc. vitreous plumbing fixtures and porcelain electrical supplies	326, x 3261, 4
32.10	Concrete products, including block and brick	3271, 2
32.11	Ready-mixed concrete	3273
32.12	Lime	3274
32.13	Gypsum products	3275
32.14	Cut stone and stone products	328
32.15	Abrasive products	3291
32.16	Asbestos products	3292
32.17	Mineral wool	3296
32.18	Nonmetallic mineral products, nec., including gaskets, packing and sealing devices, ground or treated minerals and earths, and nonclay refractories	3293, 5, 7, 9
	Primary Metal Industries	
33.01	Blast furnace and basic steel products	331
33.02	Iron and steel foundries	332
33.03	Primary copper	3331
33.04	Primary lead	3332
33.05	Primary zinc	3333
33.06	Primary aluminum	3334
33.07	Primary nonferrous metals, nec.	3339
33.08	Secondary nonferrous metals	334
33.09	Aluminum sheet, plate, and foil, aluminum extruded products, aluminum rolling and drawing, nec.	3353, 4, 5

FTC Code	Description	Related 1972 SIC or Census Codes
33.10	Nonferrous rolling and drawing (including copper), nec.	3351, 6
33.11	Nonferrous wire drawing and insulating	3357
33.12	Nonferrous foundries	336
33.13	Misc. primary metal products	339
	Fabricated Metal Products, Except Machinery and Transportation Equipment	
34.01	Metal cans	3411
34.02	Metal barrels, drums, and pails	3412
34.03	Cutlery	3421
34.04	Hand and edge tools, exc. machine tools	3423, 5
34.05	Hardware, nec.	3429
34.06	Enameled iron and metal sanitary ware	3431
34.07	Plumbing fixture fittings and trim (brass goods)	3432
34.08	Heating equipment, exc. electric and warm air furnaces	3433
34.09	Fabricated structural metal	3441
34.10	Metal doors, sash, frames, molding, and trim	3442
34.11	Fabricated plate work (boiler shops)	3443
34.12	Misc. metal work, including sheet metal, architectural and ornamental metal work, and prefabricated metal buildings and parts	3444, 6, 8, 9
34.13	Screw machine products, bolts, etc.	345
34.14	Metal forgings, ferrous and nonferrous	3462, 3
34.15	Automotive stampings	3465
34.16	Crowns and closures	3466
34.17	Metal stampings, nec.	3469
34.18	Metal coating, engraving, and allied services	347
34.19	Ordnance and accessories, exc. vehicles and guided missiles	348
34.20	Valves and pipe fittings, except plumbers' brass goods	3494

APPENDIX 3 (*Continued*)

FTC Code	Description	Related 1972 SIC or Census Codes
34.21	Misc. fabricated metal products, exc. valves and pipe fittings	349, x 3494
	Machinery Except Electrical	
35.01	Turbines and turbine generator sets	3511
35.02	Internal combustion engines, nec.	3519
35.03	Farm machinery and equipment	3523
35.04	Lawn and garden equipment	3524
35.05	Construction machinery and equipment	3531
35.06	Mining machinery and equipment, exc. oil field machinery and equipment	3532
35.07	Oil field machinery and equipment	3533
35.08	Elevators and moving stairways	3534
35.09	Conveyors and conveying equipment	3535
35.10	Hoists, industrial cranes, and monorail systems	3536
35.11	Industrial trucks, tractors, trailers and stackers	3537
35.12	Machine tools, metal cutting types	3541
35.13	Machine tool accessories and measuring devices	3545
35.14	Power driven hand tools	3546
35.15	Metalworking, machinery, nec., including metal forming machine tools, special dies and tools, die sets, jigs and fixtures, industrial molds and rolling mill machinery and equipment	3542, 4, 7, 9
35.16	Food products machinery	3551
35.17	Textile machinery	3552
35.18	Woodworking machinery	3553
35.19	Paper industries machinery	3554
35.20	Printing trades machinery	3555
35.21	Special industrial machinery, nec.	3559
35.22	Pumps and pumping equipment	3561
35.23	Ball and roller bearings	3562

FTC Code	Description	Related 1972 SIC or Census Codes
35.24	Air and gas compressors	3563
35.25	Blowers and exhaust and ventilation fans	3564
35.26	Speed changers, industrial high speed drives, and gears	3566
35.27	Industrial process furnaces and ovens	3567
35.28	Mechanical power transmission equipment, nec.	3568
35.29	General industrial machinery and equipment, nec., including industrial patterns	3565, 9
35.30	Typewriters	3572
35.31	Electronic computing equipment	3573
35.32	Calculating and accounting machines, exc. electronic computing equipment	3574
35.33	Scales and balances, exc. laboratory	3576
35.34	Office machines, nec.	3579
35.35	Air conditioning and warm air heating equipment and commercial and industrial refrigeration equipment	3585
35.36	Service industry machines, nec., including automatic merchandising machines; commercial laundry, dry cleaning, and pressing machines; and measuring and dispensing pumps	358, x 3585
35.37	Misc. machinery, except electrical	359
	Electrical and Electronic Machinery, Equipment, and Supplies	
36.01	Transformers	3612
36.02	Switchgear and switchboard apparatus	3613
36.03	Motors and generators	3621
36.04	Industrial controls	3622
36.05	Welding apparatus, electric	3623
36.06	Carbon and graphite products	3624
36.07	Electrical industrial apparatus, nec.	3629

A P P E N D I X   3   *(Continued)*

FTC Code	Description	Related 1972 SIC or Census Codes
36.08	Household cooking equipment	3631
36.09	Household refrigerators and freezers	3632
36.10	Household laundry equipment	3633
36.11	Household vacuum cleaners	3635
36.12	Household appliances, nec., including electric housewares and fans and sewing machines	3634, 6, 9
36.13	Electric lamps	3641
36.14	Residential, commercial, industrial and institutional electric lighting fixtures	3645, 6
36.15	Vehicular lighting equipment	3647
36.16	Lighting equipment, nec., including current-carrying and noncurrent-carrying wiring devices	3643, 4, 8
36.17	Radio and TV receiving sets	3651
36.18	Phonograph records	3652
36.19	Telephone and telegraph apparatus	3661
36.20	Radio and TV communication equipment	3662
36.21	Electron tubes, receiving and transmitting types	3671, 3
36.22	Cathode ray television picture tubes	3672
36.23	Semiconductors and related devices	3674
36.24	Electronic capacitors, resistors, coils and transformers, connectors and components, nec.	3675, 6, 7, 8, 9
36.25	Storage batteries	3691
36.26	Primary batteries, dry and wet	3692
36.27	Engine electrical equipment	3694
36.28	X-ray apparatus and tubes, electrical equipment and supplies, nec.	3693, 9
	Transportation Equipment	
37.01	Passenger cars	37111, 37115
37.02	Trucks	37112, pt. 3713
37.03	Buses	37113, pt. 3713

FTC Code	Description	Related 1972 SIC or Census Codes
37.04	Combat vehicles, tanks	37114, 3795
37.05	Motor vehicle parts	3714
37.06	Truck trailers	3715
37.07	Aircraft and aircraft equipment, nec.	3721, 8
37.08	Aircraft engines and engine parts	3724
37.09	Ship and boat building and repairing	373
37.10	Railroad equipment	374
37.11	Motorcycles, bicycles, and parts	375
37.12	Guided missiles, space vehicles, and parts	376
37.13	Travel trailers and campers	3792
37.14	Transportation equipment, nec.	3799
	Measuring, Analyzing, and Controlling Instruments; Photographic, Medical and Optical Goods; Watches and Clocks	
38.01	Engineering and scientific instruments	381
38.02	Measuring and controlling devices	382
38.03	Optical instruments and lenses	383
38.04	Dental equipment and supplies	3843
38.05	Surgical and medical instruments, appliances and supplies	384, x 3843
38.06	Opthalmic goods	385
38.07	Photocopying equipment	38612
38.08	Photographic equipment and supplies, exc. photocopying equipment	3861, x 38612, 38616-25, 38617-31, 32 & pt. 38618-11
38.09	Watches, clocks, and watchcases	387
	Miscellaneous Manufacturing Industries	
39.01	Jewelry, silverware, and plated ware	391
39.02	Musical Instruments	393
39.03	Sporting and athletic goods, nec.	3949
39.04	Dolls, games, toys, and children's vehicles	394, x 3949

FTC Code	Description	Related 1972 SIC or Census Codes
39.05	Pens, pencils, office and art supplies	395
39.06	Costume jewelry and notions	396
39.07	Hard surface floor coverings	3996
39.08	Misc. manufacturing, exc. hard surface floor coverings	399, x 3996
	NON-MANUFACTURING CATEGORIES:	
1.01	Agricultural production—crops	01
2.01	Agricultural production—livestock	02
7.01	Agricultural services	07
8.01	Forestry and fishing	08, 09
10.01	Metal Mining	10
11.01	Anthracite mining and bituminous coal and lignite	11, 12
13.01	Oil and gas extraction	13
14.01	Mining and quarrying of nonmetallic minerals, except fuels	14
15.01	Construction	15, 16, 17
40.01	Transportation and public utilities	40, 41, 42, 43, 44, 45, 46, 47, 48, 49
50.01	Wholesale trade	50, 51
52.01	Retail trade	52, 53, 54, 55, 56, 57, 58, 59
60.01	Finance, insurance, and real estate	60, 61, 62, 63, 64, 65, 66, 67
70.01	Services	70, 72, 73, 75, 76, 78, 79, 80, 81, 82, 83, 84, 86, 88, 89

Flowchart

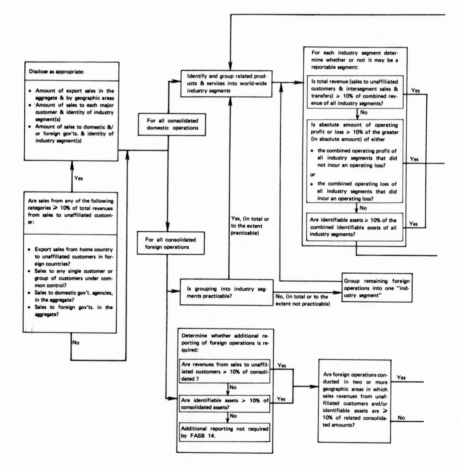

Disclose as appropriate:
• Amount of export sales in the aggregate & by geographic areas • Amount of sales to each major customer & identity of industry segment(s) • Amount of sales to domestic &/or foreign gov'ts. & identity of industry segment(s)

Identify and group related products & services into world-wide industry segments

For all consolidated domestic operations

For each industry segment determine whether or not it may be a reportable segment:

Is total revenue (sales to unaffiliated customers & intersegment sales & transfers) > 10% of combined revenue of all industry segments? — Yes

No

Is absolute amount of operating profit or loss > 10% of the greater (in absolute amount) of either
• the combined operating profit of all industry segments that did not incur an operating loss? — Yes

or

• the combined operating loss of all industry segments that did incur an operating loss?

No

Are identifiable assets > 10% of the combined identifiable assets of all industry segments? — Yes

Yes

Are sales from any of the following categories > 10% of total revenues from sales to unaffiliated customer:

• Export sales from home country to unaffiliated customers in foreign countries?
• Sales to any single customer or group of customers under common control?
• Sales to domestic gov't. agencies, in the aggregate?
• Sales to foreign gov'ts. in the aggregate?

No

For all consolidated foreign operations

Yes, (in total or to the extent practicable)

Is grouping into industry segments practicable?

No, (in total or to the extent not practicable)

Group remaining foreign operations into one "industry segment"

Determine whether additional reporting of foreign operations is required:

Are revenues from sales to unaffiliated customers > 10% of consolidated? — Yes

No

Are identifiable assets > 10% of consolidated assets? — Yes

No

Additional reporting not required by FASB 14.

Are foreign operations conducted in two or more geographic areas in which sales revenues from unaffiliated customers and/or identifiable assets are > 10% of related consolidated amounts? — Yes / No

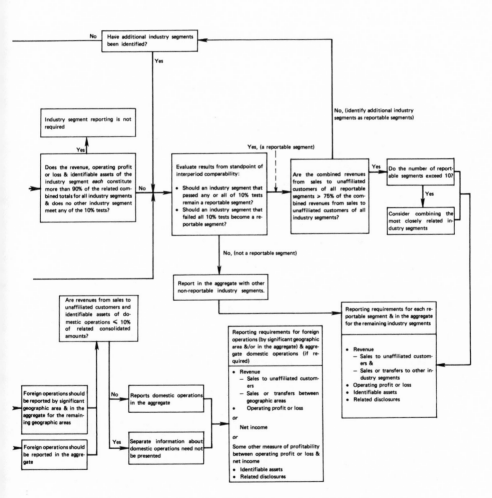

Have additional industry segments been identified?

No

Yes

Industry segment reporting is not required

Yes

No, (identify additional industry segments as reportable segments)

Yes, (a reportable segment)

Does the revenue, operating profit or loss & identifiable assets of the industry segment *each* constitute more than 90% of the related combined totals for all industry segments & does no other industry segment meet any of the 10% tests?

No

Evaluate results from standpoint of interperiod comparability:
- Should an industry segment that passed any or all of 10% tests remain a reportable segment?
- Should an industry segment that failed all 10% tests become a re-portable segment?

Are the combined revenues from sales to unaffiliated customers of all reportable segments > 75% of the combined revenues from sales to unaffiliated customers of all industry segments?

Yes

Do the number of report-able segments exceed 10?

Yes

Consider combining the most closely related in-dustry segments

No, (not a reportable segment)

Report in the aggregate with other non-reportable industry segments.

Are revenues from sales to unaffiliated customers and identifiable assets of do-mestic operations ≤ 10% of related consolidated amounts?

Reporting requirements for foreign operations (by significant geographic area &/or in the aggregate) & aggre-gate domestic operations (if re-quired)
- Revenue
  − Sales to unaffiliated custom-ers
  − Sales or transfers between geographic areas
  − Operating profit or loss

or

Net income

or

Some other measure of profitability between operating profit or loss & net income
- Identifiable assets
- Related disclosures

Reporting requirements for each re-portable segment & in the aggregate for the remaining industry segments

- Revenue
  − Sales to unaffiliated custom-ers &
  − Sales or transfers to other in-dustry segments
- Operating profit or loss
- Identifiable assets
- Related disclosures

Foreign operations should be reported by significant geographic area & in the aggregate for the remain-ing geographic areas

No

Reports domestic operations in the aggregate

Foreign operations should be reported in the aggre-gate

Yes

Separate information about domestic operations need not be presented

Flowchart **173**

Index

Tulane Symposium (1966), Tulane
University of Louisiana, 10

United States International Trade
Commission, 6
Utility costs, 36

Vertically integrated operations, 69, 75